Early
Reading First
and Beyond

*In memory of my sister, Francis (May 23, 1969–July 2, 2001).
My sister, Fran, loved children very much. Growing up she was my
best friend. She followed me to college after her study abroad
experience in France. She loved playing soccer, listening to music,
and playing her guitar. Fran would have loved to dedicate this book
to the children at the School of Inquiry where she worked
as a social worker for children most in need.*

Early Reading First and Beyond

Susan E. Israel

A Guide to Building Early Literacy Skills

CORWIN PRESS
A SAGE Company
Thousand Oaks, CA 91320

For information:

Corwin Press
A SAGE Company
2455 Teller Road
Thousand Oaks, California 91320
www.corwinpress.com

SAGE Ltd.
1 Oliver's Yard
55 City Road
London EC1Y 1SP
United Kingdom

SAGE India Pvt. Ltd.
B 1/I 1 Mohan Cooperative
   Industrial Area
Mathura Road, New Delhi
India 110 044

SAGE Asia-Pacific Pte. Ltd.
33 Pekin Street #02-01
Far East Square
Singapore 048763

Printed in the United States of America.

Library of Congress Cataloging-in-Publication Data

Israel, Susan E.
Early reading first and beyond : a guide to building early literacy skills/Susan E. Israel.
   p. cm.
Includes bibliographical references and index.
ISBN 978-1-4129-5101-2 (cloth)
ISBN 978-1-4129-5102-9 (pbk.)
   1. Reading (Early childhood) 2. Literacy. 3. Reading comprehension—Study and teaching (Early childhood)—United States. 4. Metacognition in children. I. Title.

LB1139.5.R43I84 2008
372.41—dc22   2007023148

This book is printed on acid-free paper.

07 08 09 10 11 10 9 8 7 6 5 4 3 2 1

Managing Editor:	Cathy Hernandez
Editorial Assistants:	Megan Bedell, Cathleen Mortensen
Production Editor:	Cassandra Margaret Seibel
Copy Editor:	Barbara Coster
Typesetter:	C&M Digitals (P) Ltd.
Proofreader:	Kevin Gleason
Indexer:	Holly Day
Cover Designer:	Scott Van Atta

Contents

Preface

It is the supreme art of the teacher to awaken joy in creative expression and knowledge.

Albert Einstein

My early memories of childhood experiences are the ones when I was busy playing, doing art projects, going to the library, and building things with blocks and Legos. Einstein's quote is one of my favorites because I believe creative expression and knowledge begin at a very early age in a child's cognitive, social, and emotional development.

Susan E. Israel

*E*arly Reading First and Beyond is a book about prekindergarten literacy skill development, which research shows plays a key role in a child's later success in reading achievement. The U.S. Department of Education's response to this research is the Early Reading First initiative—a program that emphasizes the importance of educating teachers who work with emerging readers. Based on the report of the National Reading Panel, Early Reading First is part of the No Child Left Behind act. The primary goal of Early Reading First—the development of literacy skills from birth to kindergarten—is the focus of this book.

What motivated me to write this book was my love for small children—all small children, not just a few—who deserve to have opportunities during vital developmental moments in their lives for those rich literacy engagements that lead to success later in life. This book provides the tools and resources for early childhood educators to unlock children's creativity to inspire them to develop readiness skills for kindergarten based on the Early Reading First initiative.

The goal of all teachers serving our young children should be to be highly qualified in their area of expertise. In addition, each teacher needs a willingness to engage in professional development for continued growth. It is my hope that by reading this book, early childhood educators will benefit from my research, experiences, and understanding of the time in a child's life from birth to kindergarten. This book will be useful as teachers reflect on their own professional development needs.

LEAVING NO EARLY CHILDHOOD EDUCATOR BEHIND

This book was written to meet the needs of educators at the emergent level who work to develop literacy for early primary grade children. The responsibility of scaffolding early primary grade children toward future literacy success does not rest in the hands of only a few people. Those who will benefit from reading this book include the following:

- Early childhood educators
- Administrators in early childhood
- Undergraduate or graduate-level professionals who teach early childhood courses in literacy and education
- School leaders who wish to engage in professional development
- Literacy coaches
- Early primary reading specialists
- School district curriculum developers
- Policymakers who work in early childhood
- Librarians who engage in literacy development activities
- Most important, parents of young children who desire to understand and implement Early Reading First goals

THINKING CREATIVELY ABOUT EARLY CHILDHOOD LITERACY DEVELOPMENT

This book offers the field of literacy a format that will appeal to those working with early childhood–age children or those who want to construct early childhood programs of excellence. It also provides teachers and parents with creative teaching that will guide their instruction related to the key components of Early Reading First. Table 0.1 provides an overview of research and strategies you will find in this book.

Detailed current research-based strategies with literacy instruction that integrate the key components presented are as follows:

- Oral language
- Alphabetic knowledge
- Phonological awareness
- Print awareness

Each chapter includes unique features to aid in developing a deeper understanding of the chapter contents for the readers. The unique features provide a consistent reading path throughout the book, making reading comprehension more efficient for the reader. These unique features are as follows:

Vignettes: An opening vignette illustrates the chapter contents and highlights key aspects of experiences in early childhood. Vignettes are provided to stimulate the reader's background knowledge on the topic.

Table 0.1   Matrix of Early Reading First Research, Strategies, and Benefits

Read This Chapter to Learn . . .	You Need to Know . . .	This Should Be Important Because . . .	The Research-Based Strategies You Can Learn About Are . . .	To Increase Home-School Connections You Can . . .
Chapter 1: Early Reading First	Goals	Pathway to change	How to self-assess	Host information workshops, listen to ideas
Chapter 2: Oral Language	How oral language develops	Oral language can be nurtured	Dialogic discussions, scaffolding statements, functions	Teach storytelling, prompts, rereading, and discussions
Chapter 3: Alphabetic Knowledge	Letter-sound connections	Predictor of later reading achievement	Mnemonic literacy, integration, reading ABC books and wordless picture books, coaching strategies	Communicate resources that are effective, teach how to use books to develop letter-sound
Chapter 4: Phonological Awareness	Segmentation, blending	Children need to master one or two skills	Multisensory approaches, elements of teaching vowels and consonants	Read-aloud strategies, teaching tips
Chapter 5: Print Awareness	Functions of a book	Increase reading prior to kindergarten	Overview books, awareness function cards	Use predictable books, watch the TV show *Between the Lions*
Chapter 6: Early Literacy Classrooms of Excellence	Cognitive, social, and emotional aspects	Impacts motivation and learning	How to use literacy tools effectively	Share talents, weekly newsletters, home service activities

Research That Early Childhood Teachers Need to Know: This section is designed to present background knowledge about each component of Early Reading First legislation or other scientifically validated components.

New Classroom-Proven Research-Based Practices: In this section, validated instructional practices address the goal of the literacy domain discussed in each chapter.

Early Reading First Assessment Tools: To meet the goals of Early Reading First, every chapter provides concrete methods that teachers can use as a screening tool for students who might be at risk for reading failure. The types of assessments recommended are brief, easy to use and interpret, administered individually or in small groups, and used to identify at-risk children. The recommended assessments are not meant to track children but to identify those at risk and to provide intervention prior to kindergarten.

Differentiating for Early Learners With Individual Needs: This unique feature describes how to make adaptations and differentiate instruction for preschool children with special needs. Chapters focus on strategies that guide teachers on how to differentiate activities.

Teaching Tips That Increase Home-School Connections: Since the inclusion of parents is a vital element in the early childhood years regarding literacy growth, this unique feature can be found in a gray box in each chapter. The tips focus on content-specific approaches that teachers can share with the parents of children in their classroom that can easily be implemented in home environments.

Literacy Treasure Chest: This unique feature can be valuable for teachers who want new ideas on specific literature that supports chapter contents.

Facilitator's Guide: At the end of the book is a helpful guide for those who want to use this book in professional development sessions or study groups. Helpful resources include Tips for Facilitators, Needs Assessments, Reproducibles, and Children's Book Lists

This book is also organized around specific standards set forth by the International Reading Association (IRA). A matrix that shows how this book connects with the IRA standards is included in Table 0.2. This table is valuable to educators working with preschool children because the specific areas of professional development you are focusing on provide you with a quick reference to specific chapters that support a standard.

In conjunction with the standards set forth by the IRA, the contents of this book answer the following questions:

Questions About Knowledge Function

What is Early Reading First, and how do I implement the components into my curriculum?

What does current research say about oral language, alphabetic principle, phonemic awareness, and higher-level thinking?

What are stages of language development and reading acquisition, and what can I do to facilitate growth?

Questions About Instructional Strategies and Curriculum

What are effective research-based strategies I can use today?

How do I respond to critical issues in early childhood programs?

What type of literature helps develop Early Reading First components, and what are some popular titles that children will enjoy?

Questions About Assessment, Diagnosis, and Evaluation

How can I evaluate my beliefs about individual aspects of Early Reading First components?

Table 0.2   Early Reading First and Beyond Chapter Correlations With IRA Standards

IRA Standard 1: Functional Knowledge	Chapters
Element 1.1 Knowledge of psychological and linguistic foundations of reading and writing processes and instruction	2, 3, 4
Element 1.2 Knowledge of reading research and histories of reading	1, 2, 3, 4, 5, 6
Element 1.3 Knowledge of language development and reading acquisition and the variations related to cultural and linguistic diversity	3, 4, 5, 6

IRA Standard 2: Instructional Strategies and Curriculum Materials	Chapters
Element 2.1 Use instructional grouping options as appropriate for accomplishing given purposes	2, 3, 4, 5, 6
Element 2.2 Use a wide range of instructional practices, approaches, and methods, including technology-based practices for learners at different stages of development and from different cultural and linguistic backgrounds	2, 3, 4, 5, 6
Element 2.3 Use a wide range of curriculum materials in effective reading instruction for learners at different stages of reading and writing development and from different cultural and linguistic backgrounds	2, 3, 4, 5, 6

IRA Standard 3: Assessment, Diagnosis, and Evaluation	Chapters
Element 3.1 Use a wide variety of assessment tools and practices that range from individual and group standardized tests to individual and group informal classroom assessment strategies, including technology-based assessment tools	2, 3, 4, 5, 6
Element 3.2 Place students along a developmental continuum and identify students' proficiencies and difficulties	1, 2, 3, 4, 5
Element 3.3 Use assessment information to plan, evaluate, and revise effective instruction that meets the needs of all students, including those at different developmental stages and those from different cultural and linguistic backgrounds	2, 3, 4, 5, 6

IRA Standard 4: Creating a Literate Environment	Chapters
Element 4.1 Use students' interests, reading abilities, and backgrounds as foundations for the reading and writing program	1, 2
Element 4.2 Use a large supply of books, technology-based information, and nonprint materials representing multiple levels, broad interests, cultures, and linguistic backgrounds	2, 3, 4, 5
Element 4.3 Model reading and writing enthusiastically as valued lifelong readers	2, 3, 4, 5, 6

IRA Standard 5: Professional Development	Chapters
Element 5.1 Display dispositions related to reading and the teaching of reading	1, 2, 3, 4, 5, 6
Element 5.2 Continue to pursue the development of professional knowledge and dispositions	1, 2, 3, 4, 5, 6
Element 5.3 Work with colleagues to observe, evaluate, and provide feedback on each other's practice	1, 6
Element 5.4 Participate in, initiate, implement, and evaluate professional development programs	1, 2, 3, 4, 5, 6

What assessments are appropriate to use with primary children?

What should the goals of assessment be in early childhood centers of excellence?

Questions About Creating a Literate Environment

What environmental factors influence early literacy growth?

How do I integrate components of early reading first in early childhood environments?

What types of home-school connections will enable higher levels of reading achievement?

Questions About Professional Development

Where can I obtain information about Early Reading First?

What are suggestions for grant writing?

What are some recommended professional development resources that will help me learn more about Early Reading First components?

After reading this book, if you have a deeper understanding of the critical developmental aspects of the key components of this book—oral language, phonological awareness, print awareness, alphabetic knowledge, and enriched early literacy environments—the goal of this book will have been achieved.

Acknowledgments

First, I wish to thank the Corwin Press staff who worked on the production of this book.

Second, I would like to thank the U.S. Department of Education for responding to my many requests to obtain the most up-to-date research on the Early Reading First initiative.

Third, I would like to thank Anne Marie Short, Youth Services Department Head at Fishers Public Library of Fishers, Indiana, for her support in gathering some of the favorite children's picture books in the library. She was instrumental in picking children's favorites for the book collections on books with names in the titles, rhyming books, and multisensory ABC books.

Publisher's Acknowledgments

Corwin Press gratefully acknowledges the contributions of the following individuals:

Richard Allington, Professor of Reading Education
University of Tennessee, Knoxville, TN

Jennifer Ramamoorthi, Professional Development School Coordinator
Community Consolidated School District 21, Palatine, IL

Catherine Compton-Lilly, Assistant Professor of Curriculum and Instruction
University of Wisconsin, Madison

About the Author

 **Susan E. Israel**, PhD, is a literacy consultant in preschool literacy materials with Burkhart Network in Indianapolis, Indiana. Her research agenda focuses on reading comprehension that pertains to all aspects of literacy such as vocabulary development, writing, and metacognition. She is a member of the National Reading Conference and the International Reading Association. She has served as the President of the History of Reading, Special Interest Group in 2006–2007. She was awarded the 2005 Panhellenic Council Outstanding Professor Award at the University of Dayton. She was the 1998 recipient of the teacher-researcher grant from the International Reading Association, where she has served and been a member for over a decade. Her authored or edited volumes include *Collaborative Literacy: Engaging Gifted Strategies for All Learners* (2006), *Shaping the Reading Field* (2007), *Poetic Possibilities: Poems to Enhance Literacy Learning* (2006), *Quotes to Inspire Great Reading Teachers* (2006), *Metacognition in Literacy Learning* (2005), *Reading First and Beyond* (2005), *Handbook of Research on Reading Comprehension* (2008), *Metacognitive Assessments* (2007), *Comprehensive Guide to Teacher Research* (2007), *The Ethical Educator* (2007), and *Dynamic Literacy Instruction* (2007).

Introduction to Early Reading First

The ultimate goal of Early Reading First is to close the achievement gap by preventing reading difficulties.

U.S. Department of Education (2006, p. 1)

When I think about my early reading experiences, I think about my visits to my grandmother's house. I could hardly wait to go to the basement and sit on her love seat and go through her basket of books. In the basket were many I Can Read! books. What I liked about this experience was that the book selections were ones that fit my reading ability—simple picture books. I also liked the ability to choose my own books. Even though I could not read the words, this early reading experience stands out in my mind as being positive and helped guide me to becoming a reader.

Susan E. Israel

What is Early Reading First (ERF)? The U.S. Department of Education's No Child Left Behind (NCLB) act has helped decrease the achievement gap by focusing on increasing literacy so all children can be highly literate. NCLB is built on four guiding principles: accountability for results, more choices for parents, greater local control and flexibility, and an emphasis on scientific research. NCLB established Reading First as a literacy policy and national program of excellence for all primary-age children in America (Block & Israel, 2005). NCLB's primary emphasis is increasing literacy so all children can have the opportunity to obtain and have access to resources to become highly literate. With the goal in mind of increasing literacy for all, the U.S. Department of Education, in conjunction with Reading First, launched a plan for the prevention of early reading difficulties called Early Reading First. ERF is aligned with NCLB. According to the U.S. Department of Education (2005), the ultimate goal of the ERF is

> to improve the school readiness of our nation's young children, especially those from low-income families, by providing support for early childhood education programs serving preschool-age children so they may become centers of educational excellence. (p. 2)

The purpose of this book is to summarize the ERF initiatives and scientific research in order to provide early childhood educators with a road map on teaching of excellence for all preschool-age children and discover how to integrate ERF components into instruction at the preschool level. This chapter answers the following questions:

- What is ERF?
- What do teachers need to know?
- What are the goals of ERF?

Early Reading First and Beyond: A Guide to Building Early Literacy Skills is written to assist preschool teachers, administrators, early literacy coaches, school district administrative staff, and parents in understanding ERF legislative initiatives and in enhancing early language and emergent literacy skills of *all* preschool-age children. This book can be used in the following ways:

1. It can be used as a professional development tool for learning about scientific reading research based on ERF legislation.

2. It can be used by early literacy educational schools that wish to improve prereading skills and more effectively collaborate with parents and caregivers of preschool-age children.

3. It can be used by educators and parents who want to learn new strategies about how to enrich all aspects of early reading experiences.

RESEARCH THAT EARLY CHILDHOOD TEACHERS CAN USE ABOUT EARLY READING FIRST

ERF is an initiative that responds to the report from the National Reading Panels (NRP) published in the fall of 2000 (National Institute of Child Health and Human Development [NICHHD], 2000). ERF was created to address the growing concern that many children enter kindergarten without the necessary foundation to develop in the area of reading and literacy.

In the following paragraphs, ERF will be defined with background information about how ERF legislation began and the overall goals of the program.

The U.S. Department of Education (2002a) defines ERF as follows:

> Early Reading First, part of the President's "Good Start, Grow Smart" initiative, is designed to transform existing early education programs into centers of excellence that provide high-quality, early education to young children, especially those from low-income families. The overall purpose of the Early Reading First Program is to prepare young children to enter kindergarten with the necessary language, cognitive, and early reading skills to prevent reading difficulties and ensure school success. (n.p.)

The Early Reading First initiative supports educational initiatives in the following ways:

1. Provides funding for low-income organizations

2. Guides preschool integration curriculums with emphasis on ERF goals

3. Offers support through government programs and resources

The U.S. Department of Education provides free resources to help increase teacher and parent knowledge on ERF. Some free titles to request are the following:

Healthy Start, Grow Smart Series (U.S. Department of Education, 2002b). Information booklets from newborn through 12 months old.

No Child Left Behind: What Parents Need to Know (U.S. Department of Education, 2006). An information booklet on how parents can increase literacy skills in the home environment.

From Risk to Opportunity: Fulfilling the Educational Needs of Hispanic Americans in the 21st Century (U.S. President's Advisory Commission on Educational Excellence for Hispanic Americans, 2003). This teacher resource explains the crisis in America and instructional strategies for intervention.

Early Reading First Goals

- Goal #1 Support:

Support efforts to enhance early language, literacy, and prereading development of preschool-age children.

- Goal #2 Cognitive Learning Opportunities:

Provide preschool-age children with cognitive learning opportunities in high-quality language and literature-rich environments so children can attain fundamental knowledge and skills necessary for optimal reading development in kindergarten and beyond.

- Goal #3 Research-Based and Age-Appropriate Instruction:

Instruction must be research based and developmentally appropriate as well as focus on oral language, phonological awareness, print awareness, and alphabetic knowledge.

- Goal #4 Assess and Identify At-Risk Preschool-Age Children:

Use screening assessments to identify preschool-age children who may be at risk for reading failure.

Preschool children are an important population and should not be overlooked in the future development of a literate America. The NCLB reform initiatives have forced educators to reflect on practice. NCLB is summarized in *Reading First and Beyond* (Block & Israel, 2005):

> NCLB is the historic, bipartisan education reform effort that President Bush proposed his first week in office and that Congress passed into law on January 8, 2002. The No Child Left Behind Act of 2001 (NCLB) reauthorized the Elementary and Secondary Education Act (ESEA)— the main federal law affecting education from kindergarten through high school. (p. 4)

In order to achieve the goals of ERF, the federal government has made available competitive awards for up to six years to support efforts that enhance early literacy reading development, especially in underresourced communities in the United States with low-income families and at-risk preschool-age children. Grants will be awarded based on the recommendation of a federal peer review panel. The panel must include experts in early reading development and early childhood education. The U.S. Department of Education awarded over $75 million to 175 preschool centers that wish to become centers of excellence. The estimated range for each grant is between $250,000 and $1.5 million. According to the U.S. Department of Education, a "center" is defined as a classroom or multiple classrooms within a building or campus, or multiple buildings. For example, it may be a Head Start center with one or more classrooms. For information about funding ideas and recommendations on the application process, see Chapter 6 in this book. An overview of how the allocated funding for ERF grants can be used is as follows:

- Professional development (knowledge of subject, classroom management, high-quality instruction, recruiting, hiring, evaluation of teacher performance, and instruction to work more effectively with parents)
- Salaries for new teachers, stipends, bonuses, scholarships, and for specialist teachers to reduce class size
- Support for parents and families
- Additional space if required to meet the purpose of the ERF
- Books and in-home literacy resources

Early childhood is a profound period for early literacy development, and prior to kindergarten, robust physical, emotional, and cognitive development occurs in preschool children. Students who enter kindergarten need to be ready for the academic challenges ahead. The difference between higher socioeconomic families when compared to lower socioeconomic families by age four is significant. Children living in impoverished areas are exposed to only 13 million words as compared to 45 million words for children living in higher socioeconomic areas. The research available on parental involvement demonstrates that parents more involved with literacy growth during the preschool years contribute to reading readiness in direct ways; this is a goal of ERF. ERF instructional initiatives do not deemphasize *play* or ignore *emotional* and *health* concerns of young children. The key word for ERF initiatives is *prevention*. Since an important part of prevention is identification of at-risk readers at the preschool level, assessment plays a critical role even prior to kindergarten.

Components to Assess Learning in Early Reading First Legislation

Identification of at-risk readers prior to the entry into kindergarten is critical to prevention of at-risk readers. Each of the chapters in this book outlines assessments that can be used to identify early literacy strengths and weaknesses and that follow characteristics supported by ERF. That is, assessments should be measures based on scientific research, should be developmentally appropriate, and should be easy to use and administer to individuals as diagnostic measures.

SUMMARY

In summary, prevention, not remediation, is the overall goal for early childhood educators. A major supporter of the ERF initiative is First Lady Laura Bush. She states, "The years from the crib to the classroom represent a period of intense language and cognitive growth. Armed with the right information, we can make sure every child learns to read and reads to learn" (U.S. Department of Education, 2001, n.p.). I invite you to begin the journey to help preschool children prepare for school success.

2

Oral Language Development

Emerging Vocabulary, Expressive Language, and Listening Comprehension

When I look back, I am so impressed again with the life-giving power of literature. If I were a young person today, trying to gain a sense of myself in the world, I would do that again by reading, just as I did when I was young.

Maya Angelou

Teaching children to express themselves is very important. Children should not fear talking, and I believe it is extremely important to create environments that value oral language and discussion, as well as a little chatter along the way. When I was working on my doctoral degree, I took a part-time job at a fitness center day care. The noise was incredible. There was always so much chatter going on. It amazed me how children interacted with each other. Children were not afraid to express themselves, especially when someone took their toy or book. That happened a lot.

Susan E. Israel

WHY TEACH ORAL LANGUAGE TO PRESCHOOL-AGE CHILDREN?

The focus of this chapter is on expressive and receptive oral language development and centers primarily on helping educators who teach emergent language development skills. Early Reading First (ERF) initiatives stress the need to guide preschool-age children in oral language development and should be one of the primary goals of child care centers, according to the U.S. Department of Education (2004). This chapter will answer the following questions:

- What is expressive and receptive language in relation to ERF teaching practices?
- What can teachers do to increase oral language in emergent readers?
- How can I use the knowledge in this chapter to assist parents in guiding young children?

Oral language is a predictor of reading ability; therefore, attention to language during the early years that emphasizes vocabulary, expressive language, and listening comprehension is critical. The research base that provides the foundational building blocks for early literacy educators who want to effectively develop oral language ability and be proud of helping "these little guys" is summarized below.

RESEARCH THAT EARLY CHILDHOOD TEACHERS NEED TO KNOW ABOUT ORAL LANGUAGE DEVELOPMENT

Harris and Hodges (1995) define "oral" as spoken utterances. The purpose of ERF is to raise the value of early childhood education to increase reading achievement by developing the oral language skills at the emergent level. This section explains what current reading and early childhood developmental research has to say about oral language development at this level, which includes the research that emphasizes vocabulary, expressive language, and listening comprehension. The U.S. Department of Education's ERF goal is for early literacy programs to seek to achieve classrooms of excellence by providing high-quality language-rich environments. In this environment, the following oral language activities are valued in order to develop increased levels of vocabulary, expressive language, and listening comprehension at an early age:

- Talk with children and engage them in conversation
- Help them name objects in their environments
- Read and reread stories
- Encourage children to recount experiences and describe ideas that are important to them
- Interact with others
- Provide opportunities for play

Oral Language Characteristics

Oral language development is evident within expressive language characteristics of infants. According to Liszkowski, Carpenter, Striano, and Tomasello (2006), 12- and 18-month-olds point in order to communicate when they want an adult to do something for them. To understand the nature of expressive language in the early stages of literacy developments, infants were tested to see if they would point at interesting stimuli unintentionally dropped by an adult or point in situations without requesting the objects for themselves. The purpose of the study was to find out what factors motivated expressive language development in the context of social needs. Findings suggest that infants point not to obtain objects for themselves but to direct attention to the object in order to communicate to the adult the location. This study helped clarify communicative language expressions at the primary stage of development and affirmed that infants point to request something they want, to obtain an interesting object, or to help an adult locate an object. Early oral language development through expressive language, like pointing, appears at the beginning stages of social oral language development.

As Botzakis and Malloy (2006) summarize in their analysis of emergent literacy oral language practices, educators should take into consideration how various cultural aspects influence oral language development within the context of early reading skills. For example, socioeconomic factors within certain cultures such as Native American and African American communities limit the availability of resources to develop oral language literacy skills. Technology is important in the development of emergent literacy, and not all groups have equal access to increase literacy-learning opportunities during crucial developmental stages.

One of the key components of early literacy successes of children prekindergarten is the role of the parent in the developmental process. In a study conducted by Bird, Reese, and Trip (2006), receptive and expressive oral language development can increase through emotional past-event conversations between the parent and the child. The study found that children have a better sense of self when parents engage in communication about past events. Children engaged in communication with parents about emotional past events were able to regulate emotion because they engaged in conversation about emotion. Self-concept and sense of self is inherent in listening comprehension and oral communication opportunities between parent and child.

The research in the area of oral language summarizes the important variables such as cultural aspects that might limit oral language growth, early childhood language expressions that provide evidence of cognitive language development, and children's development of listening comprehension through communication opportunities with parents or older adults.

NEW RESEARCH-BASED PRACTICES THAT EARLY CHILDHOOD TEACHERS CAN USE

Current research emphasizes how important oral language is in the reading and writing development of children entering kindergarten. In this section, early childhood teachers will learn about characteristics of oral language development by using an observation checklist, dialogic reading strategy, and specific strategies on how to develop oral language with home connections. The section begins with an informal self-assessment for teachers to use as a way to make decisions about their literacy instruction. Table 2.1 outlines the characteristics

Table 2.1 Early Childhood Oral Language Development Observation Checklist

Phase/Approximate Age	Defining Features to Observe	Instructional Intervention
4–7 Months	__ Child is listening to others talking and watches how they are communicating __ Pays attention to tone of voices: soft voices, child reacts by being calmed; loud voices, child reacts by crying __ Babies produce sounds in the form of cooing or crying. They will raise and lower their tone just like adults	Encourage conversations If a noticeable word or syllable is uttered, repeat it back Sounds like "a" introduce them to words and objects that have that sound: "apple," "ant"
6–12 Months	__ Child vocalizes pictures of pets or sounds __ Points for books	Lots of animal board books available Books available in the environment Toys that make sounds Introduce to simple words and sounds starting first with the sounds the baby makes
12–24 Months	__ Child is exhibiting oral listening comprehension skills by responding to instructions __ Uses less baby talk __ Knows names of familiar people __ Talks in short sentences __ Knows about 50 words __ Begins asking questions	Speak slowly and clearly to get attention Use less baby talk Help by teaching to talk in sentences Keep a list of words child knows and form more words using the known vocabulary Encourage questioning but ask why to let the child explain further before responding
2–3 Years	__ Uses pronouns such as "I," "me," "we" __ Talks using longer sentences __ Child might have noticeable developmental problems with language	Read shorter books to allow for attention span Encourage child to correct incomplete sentences by modeling Early detection for hearing and recommend language treatment
3–4 Years	__ Child possesses a vocabulary of about 300 words __ Imitates adults __ Chattering constantly __ Uses pronouns correctly in sentences	Encourage vocabulary development and repeating of new words by practicing them in a sentence Model using descriptive words to increase vocabulary development Ask to retell familiar stories in own words Permit child to speak for himself or herself
4–5 Years	__ Child can pronounce most sounds in the English language __ Vocabulary of about 1,500 words __ Uses complex sentences __ Attempts to use power of words to fulfill needs	Encourage appropriate use of language when asking for things Teach songs or limericks rather than mindless chatter Encourage recitation of poetry

SOURCES: Reach Out and Read National Reading Center, 2000; American Academy of Pediatrics, 2000.

Table 2.1a Israel Oral Language Observation Checklist

Behaviors to Look For	*Observation*
Behaviors during group discussions	
When I am giving directions I notice	
Feels comfortable to ask questions or seek help when necessary	
Engages in conversations with peers	
Acknowledges adult presence	
Talks to self rather than peers	
Likes to tell stories	
Other observations	

Child Observed _____   **Date of Assessment** _____

_____ Communication strengths

_____ Suggestions to consider for further development

_____ What parents might try to help

of oral language developmental patterns in children aged newborn through kindergarten. The purpose of this observation is to create a starting point for the oral language patterns and offer suggestions about instructional intervention. Use the following observation checklist to identify oral language behaviors.

The brief observation assessment in Table 2.1 can provide immediate feedback on the oral language development of a child. Table 2.1a is an adaptation for teachers to use. It is important to remember that the purpose of ERF is the early detection and intervention of children who might be at risk. Teachers of excellence who work with early preschool-age children understand that early readiness of language development is critical prior to kindergarten. Below are two intervention strategies that include sample lessons using children's literature, which can be used in the classroom to promote early language development. The strategies are meant to provide research-based ideas on how to increase oral language development, but are only considered recommendations, as with all the strategies in this book. Modifications by teachers are recommended based on their knowledge of the students within their care.

Strategy #1 Interactive Oral Reading

Interactive oral language development can be done by inviting children to participate in read-aloud experiences. Doyle and Bramwell (2006) studied the effects of dialogic reading in children ages two to six years old. Dialogic reading involves active participation in dialogue between reader and listener(s) and involves the following steps:

- Multiple reading of book
- Conversations about books with children
- Storytelling that might deviate from text to tell a story
- Prompting with questioning that encourages children to say more
- Encouraging feedback from all children to other children's responses

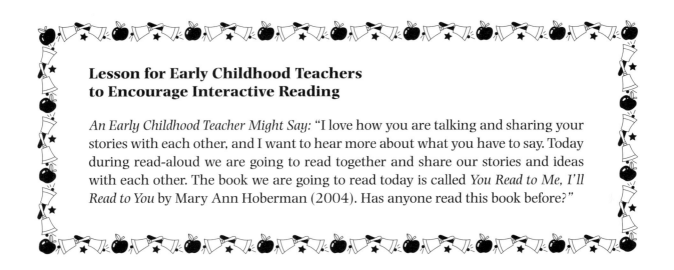

Lesson for Early Childhood Teachers to Encourage Interactive Reading

An Early Childhood Teacher Might Say: "I love how you are talking and sharing your stories with each other, and I want to hear more about what you have to say. Today during read-aloud we are going to read together and share our stories and ideas with each other. The book we are going to read today is called *You Read to Me, I'll Read to You* by Mary Ann Hoberman (2004). Has anyone read this book before?"

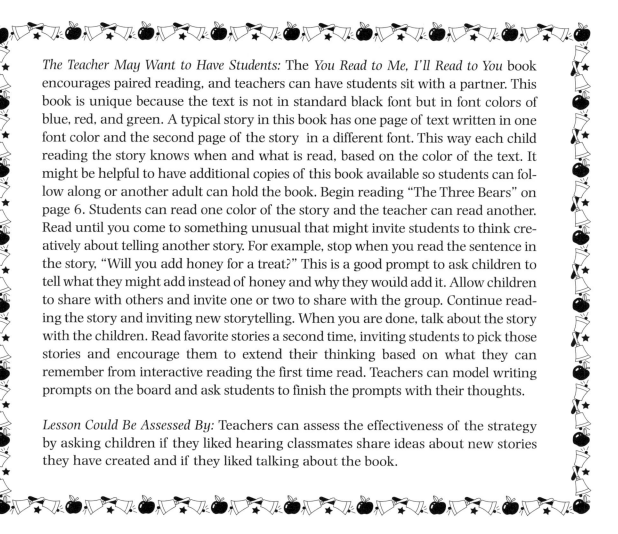

The Teacher May Want to Have Students: The *You Read to Me, I'll Read to You* book encourages paired reading, and teachers can have students sit with a partner. This book is unique because the text is not in standard black font but in font colors of blue, red, and green. A typical story in this book has one page of text written in one font color and the second page of the story in a different font. This way each child reading the story knows when and what is read, based on the color of the text. It might be helpful to have additional copies of this book available so students can follow along or another adult can hold the book. Begin reading "The Three Bears" on page 6. Students can read one color of the story and the teacher can read another. Read until you come to something unusual that might invite students to think creatively about telling another story. For example, stop when you read the sentence in the story, "Will you add honey for a treat?" This is a good prompt to ask children to tell what they might add instead of honey and why they would add it. Allow children to share with others and invite one or two to share with the group. Continue reading the story and inviting new storytelling. When you are done, talk about the story with the children. Read favorite stories a second time, inviting students to pick those stories and encourage them to extend their thinking based on what they can remember from interactive reading the first time read. Teachers can model writing prompts on the board and ask students to finish the prompts with their thoughts.

Lesson Could Be Assessed By: Teachers can assess the effectiveness of the strategy by asking children if they liked hearing classmates share ideas about new stories they have created and if they liked talking about the book.

Strategy #2 Read-Aloud Modeling to Develop Oral Language

Working with parents is a critical aspect of exemplary early childhood programs. Parents and home involvement are a bridge to literacy success (Strickland, 2004). As Strickland states, "True reading involves understanding" (p. 87). To increase family involvement and at the same time oral language development, begin at an early age in helping children and parents learn how to increase background knowledge prior to literacy experiences or read-alouds. During a parent-child activity, invite parents to bring a read-aloud from home. Before reading the book, use magazines to cut out pictures of all the things the child and parent think the book might be about, based on what they know from the title. Use the collage to share with the class prior to reading the story. During the read-aloud, model for parents how to do the following types of oral reading strategies (Block & Israel, 2004; Waldbart, Meyers, & Meyers, 2006).

Before Reading Aloud:

- Have child talk about front and back of book and illustrations
- Have child talk about how the book related to the pictures on the collage
- Have child look at pictures in the book and talk about them

During Reading Aloud:

- Ask child to explain what has happened in the story and if it makes sense
- Ask child to recall other books or experiences that might be similar to the events in the story
- Invite child to ask questions while you are reading

After Reading Aloud:

- Ask child if he or she liked the story and why or why not
- Invite to use the collage as a prompt to make up a different ending
- Show children nonfiction stories related to the same topic in the book and ask them if they are familiar with the information in the nonfiction books

Integrating Oral Language Skills Using Think-Alouds With Nonfiction Text: Oral Practice Lesson

During read-alouds, you can use prompts to reinforce oral language functions. You might say,

- I think this character is important because . . .
- I wonder why the author . . .
- I recall something like this that happened to me . . .
- I like . . .
- Where the story is taking place reminds me of a time . . .
- I think you are wondering why . . .

Following is an example of how a challenging nonfiction book, *Leonardo, Beautiful Dreamer* (Donnelly, 2003), can be used with four- to five-year-olds to stimulate conversation and inquiry. If teachers want to use this book with younger children, it is recommended it be used for children to explain the beautiful illustrations to develop oral language and introduce them to the genre of nonfiction. Prior to beginning this activity, you can distribute the previously cited sentence starters, one per student, on sentence strips.

Example of teacher scaffolding statements for the sentence fun lesson:

Teacher says: "I am going to give you three examples of responses to the sentences I gave you. Here are my responses to the three questions I selected."

1. I wonder why Leonardo left his village of Vinci to join his father in Florence?

2. I think you were wondering about Florence before I started to read the story.

3. I wish I knew why Leonardo had trouble finishing his many projects that he started, because I have trouble finishing some of my projects too.

Teacher says: "To help you speak to express your ideas and thoughts (Personal Function), I am going to demonstrate how I use my oral language to express my thoughts. I'll tell you what I think as I read and how I shape the words I want to say to tell others these thoughts."

Teacher reads the following: "More than 500 years ago, a remarkable child was born near the town of Vinci in the sun-drenched Italian countryside."

Teacher thinks aloud: "I was thinking that I can't imagine living 500 years ago. Since I was born in January, I know that the weather in the winter is very cold. When Leonardo was born, however, the weather must have been warm, because the author talks about the sun-drenched countryside. The next thought I had was: 'I wonder if my mom wishes I would have been born in warmer weather,' and 'I wish I knew more about Italy and the different seasons.'"

Teacher says: "I would like you to find a partner, and while you are reading the next few pages of Leonardo, Beautiful Dreamer, I would like you to practice expressing your ideas by saying one of the sentence starters that I modeled for you. Complete the sentence by telling your friend all about an idea you had as you read."

Oral language development is critical for early childhood literacy success in school. The more opportunities to develop oral language, the more confident the child will be about using language. Early educators should take advantage of every opportunity to develop vocabulary with children. Using similar words to describe things or using same sounds to think of other words helps increase vocabulary. In Block and Israel (2005), the main goal of oral language was to increase the amount of productive time spent reading to children.

EARLY READING FIRST ASSESSMENT TOOLS FOR ORAL LANGUAGE DEVELOPMENT

Assessment Name: Test for Early Language Development-3rd Edition (TELD-3)

Assessment Goal: To identify children's receptive and expressive language skills, measure comprehension ability and expression for individuals ages two to eight.

How to Administer: The measurement is only administered individually, with no time limit parameters; therefore, children will have limited anxiety during testing.

SOURCE: Hresko & Hammill, 1999.

Assessment Name: Oral and Written Language Scales (OWLS)

Assessment Goal: Designed to assess receptive and expression language skills for children and young adults. Lexical skills in vocabulary are assessed along with syntactical and supralinguistic skills of higher-order thinking. This assessment can be used to identify early language disabilities and assist in intervention planning.

How to Administer: This assessment is individually administered and is considered to be a valid and reliable norm-referenced assessment. Examiner follows an administration guide with item-by-item directions on how to use the laminated cards. The test is not timed.

SOURCE: Carrow-Woolfolk, 1995.

Assessment Name: Expressive Vocabulary Test (EVT)

Assessment Goal: Screens for expressive language problems and early language development, measures word retrieval ability, understanding reading problems, monitoring growth, and evaluating English language acquisition if primary language is not English.

How to Administer: The assessment is untimed and takes under 20 minutes to complete. It is used with primary-age children with starting assessment points based on age.

SOURCE: Williams, 1997.

DIFFERENTIATING FOR EARLY LEARNERS WITH INDIVIDUAL NEEDS

Early Learners Who Excel With Support

At a young age when children are beginning to develop oral language skills, it is important to use positive reinforcement at all times. Current reading research in education is focusing on how educators respond to children and the impact on achievement and self-confidence (Johnston, 2004). When speaking with children who might exhibit early oral language problems, focus on positive communication by using the following guidelines:

- I love the way you are listening to one another.
- Does anyone have any positive things they noticed about what they heard from others?
- Did anyone say something today that made you think differently?
- I like what you just said, that reminded me of something else I . . .

Early learners who might be struggling with language also need positive reinforcement, and the language of the teacher and the words chosen scaffold how they think of themselves and others.

Early Learners Who Are Learning English

The culture of schools is changing, and the more knowledge early childhood educators have about the culture of their students, the more informed they can be in ways to help students develop oral language. For students who are beginning to learn, English teachers can provide social opportunities so they can interact and learn language from their peers. Encourage parents to plan special play dates with English-speaking children. Using books on tape or interactive storybook CD-ROMS will also help English language learners. Since it is important for children to learn songs and rhymes, one children's book that also comes with a CD is *A Child's Introduction to Poetry* by Michael Driscoll (2003). The book gives teachers helpful teaching tips with each poem. All the poems in the book are also read on the CD by famous people representing a variety of cultures and dialects.

Early Learners Who Excel

Oral language ability is not the only predictor of later reading achievement (Ediger, Wilcutt, & Bohn, 2005). Immersion in print is recommended for young children who exhibit higher levels of oral language development. As suggested earlier, nonfiction text can increase curiosity and vocabulary, especially with early learners who excel. Table 2.2 summarizes a list of nonfiction books that teachers will find useful for advanced children. Table 2.3 provides a matrix of text features. Teachers can use the matrix to point out to children the difference in text format. Attention to features of nonfiction text is important for later motivation and readability development.

It is highly recommended that more emphasis be placed on using informational text in the primary grades (Duke, 2000). When in school, children begin to develop a dislike for nonfiction text because it is primarily only used to explain content and learn information. Prior to entering, schoolchildren need to develop an interest and an introduction to nonfiction text in positive ways so they can better understand the purpose for reading them, that is, to gain information (Galda & Liang, 2003). When choosing nonfiction texts, teachers should try to select text appropriate to cognitive levels of ability. Teachers should also learn about the varying functional text features in information text (Saul & Dieckman, 2005). Understanding the elements of information text will also help early childhood teachers explain to students how to read nonfiction text. For example, Pappas (2006) summarized elements of nonfiction text in order to help primary children connect science learning with language learning. As explained by Pappas, "The goal is to create a scheme that captures both variant as well as invariant properties" (p. 230). Important elements of the nonfiction genre that teachers need to know in order to help children make metacognitive connections within the text are as follows:

- Understand how to explain the purpose of prelude
- Overview with children the type of topic presentation and the format for engagement on the topic

Table 2.2   Nonfiction Children's Picture Books

1. *An Egg Is Quiet* by Dianna Aston (2006). San Francisco, CA: Chronicle Books. A book about eggs and how they turn into birds. All different types of eggs in beautiful illustrations. The font is large and easy for children to read. Different eggs are discussed throughout the book.

2. *Chicks & Chickens* by Gail Gibbons (2003). New York: Holiday House. Gail Gibbons is a very famous nonfiction children's book author. The text explains facts about chickens and their behaviors and features. The language is written in a story-type format with definitions used as labels near the pictures. The nonfiction story format explains how different cultures through history fed and raised chickens.

3. *Grizzly Bears* by Gail Gibbons (2003). New York: Holiday House. Gibbons, in keeping with her traditional informational text, manages to tell the history and behaviors of grizzly bears. Many of the pages have pictures within pictures that elaborate more fully on the facts of grizzly bears.

4. *Catching the Moon: A Story of a Young Girl's Baseball Dream* by Crystal Hubbard (2005). New York: Lee & Low Books. A story about a girl named Marcenia Lyle who loves baseball. She faces challenges that African American women face when trying to enter an all-male team. She also has to overcome challenges with her parents, who want her to enjoy school and do what most girls do.

5. *Great Crystal Bear* by Carolyn Lesser (1996). Orlando, FL: Harcourt Brace. The nonfiction writing style is done in a poetic form, with each verse giving factual information about the great crystal bear. Lots of descriptive language is used to explain factual information.

6. *Marvelous Mattie: How Margaret E. Knight Became an Inventor* by Emily Arnold McCully (2006). New York: Farrar, Straus, Giroux. The nonfiction text is perfect to provide women in science role models for young children. What is nice about the pages in this book is that at the bottom the pictures are detailed drawings of the projects that Margaret created and can easily be duplicated by children with adult support.

7. *Me Llamo Gabriela (My Name Is Gabriela)* by Monica Brown (2005). Flagstaff, AR: Luna Rising. This nonfiction book is written with English and Spanish translations on each page. It is about a girl named Gabriela Mistral who grew up in Chile. Gabriela loved words. She taught herself to read, and she also loved to write poems. She grew up to follow her dream of being a teacher in Chile.

8. *Garden of the Spirit Bear: Life in the Great Northern Rainforest* by Dorothy Hinshaw Patent (2004). New York: Clarion Books. What's unique about this small children's picture book is that it has a table of contents. This book can easily be read as a read-aloud, and children can select topics they want to learn about.

9. *Poetry for Young People: Langston Hughes,* edited by David Roessel and Arnold Rampersad (2006). New York: Sterling. The picture book begins with the life of Langston Hughes. This information is great to use to help children build background knowledge on the writer of the poems. Each poem is written by Langston Hughes but includes beautiful illustrations. At the bottom of each page are facts about things mentioned in the poem.

10. *Let Them Play* by Margot Theis Raven (2005). Chelsea, MI: Sleeping Bear Press. This nonfiction story talks about the only all-African American youth baseball team in South Carolina known as the Cannon Street league. The team faced many challenges in an all-white community. This is a riveting story about a magnificent coach and true American hero for children. This story brought tears to my eyes.

11. *Play, Mozart, Play!* by Peter Sís (2006). New York: Greenwillow Books. Mozart is a young boy whose father made him practice all the time. Few words on each page tell a story of a little boy who wants to play instead.

12. *Wings of Light: The Migration of the Yellow Butterfly* by Stephen Swinburne (2006). Honesdale, PA: Boyds Mills Press. A colorful book that tells the story of the monarch butterfly migration. The butterflies have to cross the ocean and find rest on ocean vessels. The story includes an author's note that explains interesting facts about the butterflies.

13. *Liberty Rising: The Story of the Statue of Liberty* by Pegi Deitz Shea (2005). New York: Henry Holt. Children will find this story interesting and will also learn about a career as an architect. Information about the French architect provides interesting details of how the Statue of Liberty was constructed.

Table 2.3   Matrix of Nonfiction Children's Picture Books Organizational Features

Book #	Organizational Features	Picture Format	Text Style
1	Picture Glossary	Variety of small and large photos with factual text close by	Random in lines, circles, nontraditional format
2	Heading, How-to Pages in Back, Photo Facts	Lots of diagrams with factual labels all over page	Text from left to right and labels, thought bubbles
3	Heading, How-to Pages in Back, Photo Facts	Lots of diagrams with factual labels all over page	Text from left to right and labels, thought bubbles
4	Afterword	Paintings of real-life images of faces and environment	Traditional left to right
5	Just text	Lots of diagrams with factual labels all over page	Poetry format
6	Author's Notes	Real-life paintings with diagrams on the bottom of the pages	Traditional left to right
7	Biographical Summary	Traditional Spanish scenes of people and environment	Traditional left to right
8	Maps, Resources, Index	Natural settings in forest	Traditional left to right by topics
9	Introduction, Index	Expressive dramatic photos of people	Poetry format with integration of facts randomly placed
10	Epilogue, Facts Page	Family setting and in natural setting	Traditional left to right
11	Biographical Summary	Variety of creative formats such as circles, repeated shapes, close-up shots, with text near pictures	Some text left to right, some labels, one or two words enlarged
12	Author's Notes	Lots of diagrams with factual labels all over page	Traditional left to right
13	Author's Notes, More Facts	Unusual perspectives and close-up photos	Traditional left to right

- Explain how the characteristics of events related to the topic are presented
- Understand if the information is an explanation of a topic or comparison of other pieces of information on similar topics
- Provide any historical background knowledge
- Use summary statements about the information that speak to the purpose or goal of reading the book
- Describe extra features at the end of the book and the purpose for inclusion and how this information helps with reading and comprehension ability
- Overview any extension of illustrations
- Understand how to utilize narrative or nonnarrative dialogue bubbles

TEACHING TIPS THAT INCREASE HOME-SCHOOL CONNECTIONS

- During parent night, demonstrate interactive reading methods for parents so they understand how to read to their children. Model using children and parent volunteers (Doyle & Bramwell, 2006).
- Share the teacher observation checklist with parents and include this in their parent packet at the beginning of a school year or when they register for services. Invite the parents to complete the observation checklist periodically throughout the school year.
- Teach oral language prompts that can be used with nonfiction text and encourage parents to use both nonfiction and fiction books on the same topic together.
- Share strategies for storytelling and discussions

LITERACY TREASURE CHEST

Learn more effective and interactive read-aloud methods that encourage oral language development, build vocabulary, and increase oral listening comprehension skills. To help build vocabulary, use simple rhyming books. Even if children are still in the infancy stages of literacy development, rhyming books

Table 2.4   Interactive Rhyming Books for Young Children to Enhance Oral Language

Five Little Ducks by Ivan Bates (2006). New York: Orchard Books. A fresh book about a mother duck and her babies. Use this book with nonfiction text on ducks and nature.

I'm a Duck! by Teri Sloat (2006). New York: Penguin. This book tells a story and uses sounds and features to explain what he looks like and sounds like. This book can be used to teach vocabulary and big words to advanced learners.

Wynken, Blynken, & Nod: A Poem by Eugene Field (1995). New York: North-South Books. This classic poem is done in wonderful illustrations and will calm any busy bunch of children.

Barnyard Banter by Denise Fleming (1994). New York: Henry Holt. A bright book by a famous children's author will excite any young reader who loves to rhyme words. Use this book on a field trip to a zoo or farm.

Mother Goose Favorites by Tomie dePaola (1985). New York: Penguin Books. This famous children's author illustrates popular nursery rhymes. This book can be used to help children remember rhyming words.

Chelsea Morning by Joni Mitchell (2004). New York: Simon & Schuster. This book comes with a CD that has the lyrics by this famous songwriter and singer. A wonderful book to use for auditory learning.

A Frog in the Bog by Karma Wilson (2003). New York: Simon & Schuster. A rhyming book with beautiful natural illustrations about a frog who gets bigger and has fun in the process.

The Eensy-Weensy Spider by Mary Ann Hoberman (2000). New York: Little, Brown. This book has the song and hand motions for this favorite childhood rhyme. Prior to reading this story, let children do a picture-walk to tell their own story about the spider. The illustrations are a must-see, and children will want to savor them again and again.

are a wonderful way to allow children to hear words. Adults can create new rhyming words during reading to encourage oral language creativity. Table 2.4 provides a list of wonderful children's picture books with beautiful illustrations and rhyming words.

SUMMARY

Oral language can be developed in young children. Engage in conversations with other colleagues about oral language. What are they doing to enhance oral language development? How are they aware of the cultural and socioeconomic factors within your community? What oral language development and specific intervention techniques do they use? How do they encourage expressive and receptive oral language skills at an early age?

3

Alphabetic Knowledge

Small opportunities are often the beginning of great enterprises.

Demosthenes

I was having a conversation with a mother who was sending her child to kindergarten in the fall. She asked me how she could help her child learn letters of the alphabet. Prior to her asking me this question, she was telling me how much her child loved to play in the pool they had just purchased. Since I knew the child loved water, I suggested using ABC sponges that can be purchased at most craft stores. I explained that the sponges would make a great pool toy and inspire the child to learn alphabet letters and sounds. In this chapter, ideas on assessments that can be used to detect early concerns related to the development of the alphabetic principle are provided.

Susan E. Israel

Children's early reading experiences happen in the home. According to Harris and Hodges (1995), the alphabetic principle is "the assumption underlying alphabetic writing systems that each speech sound or phoneme of a language should have its own distinctive graphic representation" (p. 7). More clearly, Stahl, Duffy-Hester, and Dought-Stahl (1998) define the alphabetic principle as letters in words that stand for specific sounds. This chapter answers the following questions:

- What do early childhood educators need to know about the alphabetic principle?
- How can parents foster the alphabetic principle at home?
- How can educators work with children to increase early literacy skills?
- What high-quality literature can I use to help nurture the alphabetic principle?

RESEARCH THAT EARLY CHILDHOOD TEACHERS NEED TO KNOW ABOUT ALPHABETIC KNOWLEDGE

In this section, you will learn about the three developmental stages of the alphabetic principle. You will also learn how to integrate the stages when planning curriculum in early childhood programs. In addition, you will also understand the position of the National Reading Panel (NRP) and International Reading Association (IRA) on early literacy development and the alphabetic principle. This information is beneficial to early childhood programs because it provides a benchmark on how to evaluate existing programs and how to use this information to increase home-school connections.

Stages of Alphabetic Principle

The NRP supports the position that phonics should be taught in the early grades. Approaches on how the alphabetic principle is integrated into the literacy program are based on the mission and goals of the school. Early childhood centers of excellence integrate alphabetic principle in literacy, not treat it as an isolated skill.

According to Ehri (1995), children develop the alphabetic principle through stages. Table 3.1 summarizes the stages and provides assessment and activities at each stage. Early childhood educators may observe the following stages in children's alphabetic principle knowledge:

Stage 1 Prealphabetic: Children can recognize words using visual cues. Teachers should use programs that have picture, sound, and letter relationships. What teachers can do to help develop prealphabetic skills is to use flashcards that show pictorial cues for letters of the alphabet. See Figure 3.1 later in this chapter for an example of such a flashcard.

Stage 2 Phonetic Cue Reading: Children begin to use partial sound recognition in words such as initial sounds or final sounds.

Stage 3 Full Alphabetic: Children are using all letters of a word to try to make sense of the word.

How to Emphasize the Alphabetic Principle

Learning the ABCs becomes one of the first literacy goals of educators and parents. Likewise, one of the earliest milestones for a child is the ability to recite

Table 3.1   Application of Stages in Early Childhood Programs

Alphabetic Stage	Behaviors to Assess	Activities
Stage 1 Prealphabetic	Can identify letter and sound with a visual cue	Use games and toys with letter-sound relationships. Use multisensory approaches to experience using different learning styles
Stage 2 Phonetic cue reading	When given a familiar word, such as a name or object known in vocabulary, will be able to identify initial letter and sound	Use repetition in words, read rhyming books, invite children to create their own rhymes using the familiar sound
Stage 3 Full alphabetic	Child is able to understand words are made up of sounds and attempt to use all the letters and sounds to say a word	When reading stories, do picture-walks first, and during the read-aloud, stop to see if children can say the next word in the text. Have children describe pictures and the words they might find in the book, write down the words, and say them together

the alphabet. Early Reading First (ERF) initiatives emphasize the development of alphabetic knowledge prior to entering kindergarten. Teachers that emphasize the alphabetic principle would seek to achieve the following:

- A print-rich environment
- A clear display of letters of the alphabet at children's eye level
- Centers that encourage language play with letters of the alphabet
- Integration of alphabetic knowledge in reading and writing opportunities
- A variety of books on display and readily available for students to look at
- Games that reinforce the alphabetic principle
- Big books on display so children can visualize words and sounds while the teacher reads aloud. See Photograph 3.1 for a method to display big books during read-alouds
- Music integrated with language arts curriculum to help learn the alphabet letters and sounds

NEW RESEARCH-BASED PRACTICES THAT EARLY CHILDHOOD TEACHERS CAN USE

One of the important recommendations that the position statement of the IRA makes on literacy development in the preschool years is that educators take

Photo 3.1   Books on Display for Children to Read

professional development seriously and work collaboratively with the home environment. This section begins with an informal self-assessment for teachers to take prior to reading the rest of the chapter and to assess their own understanding of how the alphabetic principle looks on the developmental continuum. This checklist can be used to make home-school connections with parents to help them understand what they can do at home to help their child develop alphabetic knowledge. Table 3.2 outlines the characteristics of the alphabetic principle.

What did you learn about your instruction from Table 3.2? Did you see some behaviors emerging more than others for the children you work with? Working with children on the alphabetic principle can be easily integrated with literacy activities such as mnemonic integration, using wordless picture books to increase alphabet knowledge, and strategies on how to respond to children while learning letters and sounds.

Using Letter-Sound Flashcards

By the time young children enter kindergarten, they have an awareness of the letter-sound relationships. Early childhood educators can increase alphabetic achievement by using mnemonics as a form of early decoding skill development. According to Pressley (2006), in order to help alleviate memory demands in learning letters and sounds, children can be presented with pictorial representations of a letter and sound. For example, during read-aloud experiences, teachers can use flash cards that show letters of the alphabet and corresponding pictures.

Table 3.2   Early Childhood Alphabetic Principle Observation Checklist

Approximate Age	Defining Features to Observe	Instructional Intervention
4–7 Months	__ Responds to name	Repeat beginning sounds in name and letters
6–12 Months	__ Able to say initial sounds of certain objects	Use objects that are familiar and write the letters and say the letter-sound correspondence
12–24 Months	__ Usually enjoys puzzles or hands on objects	Offer ABC puzzles, stencils, or hands-on objects that are related to multisensory approaches to learning letters and sounds
2–3 Years	__ Will understand simple questions	Ask to rename objects that are familiar Show how to trace alphabet letters using large stencils
3–4 Years	__ Makes repetitions of words and sounds	Use lots of ABC books for reading and learning words and letters of the alphabet and their sounds Use stamps to practice making letters or words from environmental print objects
4–5 Years	__ Begins to know vowels and consonants	Practice writing letters and words, use music and computer software to reinforce letters and sounds

SOURCE: Reach Out and Read National Reading Center, 2000; American Academy of Pediatrics, 2000.

Figure 3.1   Letter-Sound Flashcard

Wordless Picture Book Alphabet Writing

Several studies researched the relationship of early reading skills and comprehension processes. Paris and Paris (2003) investigated the effects of wordless picture books on comprehension instruction. The findings suggest that teachers can use wordless picture books to prompt higher-level thinking and narrative comprehension in young children. In order to develop comprehension of letter-sound relationships, Sylva and Alves-Martins (2002) found that writing can increase memory of alphabetic knowledge for letters and sounds. Through writing, children are able to "comprehend" and internalize relationships. Early childhood educators can use this research to increase alphabetic knowledge with young children by having them look at and read wordless picture books. Children can identify pictures that begin with specific letters of the alphabet and write down that corresponding letter. Teachers can participate by writing the rest of the word for the child. To encourage memory of letter-sound relationships, teachers can follow the lesson below.

Lesson for Early Childhood Teachers to Develop Alphabetic Knowledge

Teachers can use the following text: *The Red Book* by Barbara Lehman (2004).

An Early Childhood Teacher Might Say: "Today we are going to read a story. The problem is that this story has no words. The name of our book is called *The Red Book*. The type of book we are going to read is called a wordless picture book. How many of you have read a wordless picture book? After we look at the pictures on the first page, I want you to take time to find something familiar to you. What is the name of that object? Now take your crayons and let us write the first letter of that word. Now you try."

The Teacher May Want to Have Students: Children can try to write the first letter of the object they have identified. If you are working one-on-one with a child, you can finish writing the word by adding the rest of the letters and saying the letter and making each sound. For example, "On the first page in the story, I see a boy. The first sound in the word boy is /b/ and the letter is *b*. Now write the letter for the sound /b/. I will finish that word for you by adding the rest of the letters. You follow with me by pointing at the letters while I write them. The second letter is *o*. I will write the letter *o*. What sound do you hear? The last letter is *y*. I will write the letter *y*. What sound does that make? Let's read the whole word together. Can you ask a question about the boy in the picture?" The teacher can continue reading the book in this manner. When the story is complete, ask the child to retell the story using the letters and words of familiar objects in the book.

Lesson Could Be Assessed By: Teachers can assess this lesson by asking the child to identify the letters of the words that were written and the sound each letter makes.

Making Decisions About What to Say Besides "Sound It Out" or "Let Me Tell You"

Deciding what to do when a child is having difficulty is a decision educators face daily. When it comes to learning about the alphabet, our instincts tell us to provide assistance as needed and in most cases telling the students the answers. For example, if a child is having difficulty remembering what the letter *b* sounds like, we initially want to respond /b/ like in boy. Table 3.3 provides early childhood educators with action cue cards they can use when working with children. The cue cards can also be used at home to increase the home-school connections on how to help children learn letter-sound relationships in a consistent manner. Action cue cards are meant to help educators prompt a reading action to provide readers with more detailed information about the letter or word-recognition task. Action cues focus on the grapheme-phoneme, larger word parts, and contextual supports for more skilled early readers. Teachers should use discretion when using certain prompts, taking into consideration individual ability levels.

The alphabetic principle is an important first step in helping a child learn to read. The strategies presented in this chapter can easily be modified for learners with special needs. Research recommends that all the strategies be integrated with other literacy activities.

EARLY READING FIRST ASSESSMENT TOOLS FOR KNOWLEDGE OF ALPHABETIC PRINCIPLE

Assessment Name: Adult/Child Interactive Reading Inventory (ACIRI)

Assessment Goal: An observational tool for parents to use to assess beginning letter-sound identification behaviors of their child. Easily scored and administered (Rueda & Yaden, 2006)

How to Administer: The observation inventory consists of a list of storybook reading behaviors that detect early reading difficulties. The parent can administer the exam anywhere. The observation instrument can be used in culturally diverse homes.

SOURCE: DeBruin-Parecki, 1999.

Assessment Name: The Names Test of Decoding

Assessment Goal: Identify letter-sound patterns with older readers ages four to five who can read letters

How to Administer: This assessment is easy to administer and usually takes about 10 to 15 minutes. Should be given individually. Names are used because children are familiar with them in their listening vocabulary.

SOURCE: Cunningham, 2000.

Table 3.3   Preschool Cue Cards for Alphabetic Knowledge Development With Emerging Readers

Action Coaching Cue Card #1 What do you think that *letter* sounds like?	*Action Coaching Cue Card #2* It's a ___ letter sound?	*Action Coaching Cue Card #3* Is there an object in the story that you know?
Action Coaching Cue Card #4 Can you point to the letter you know?	*Action Coaching Cue Card #5* Do you see other words with some of the same letters?	*Action Coaching Cue Card #6* What in the picture starts with the same sound?
Action Coaching Cue Card #7 This is what you said . . . Does that sound right?	*Action Coaching Cue Card #8* Does this sound make sense to you?	*Action Coaching Cue Card #9* Let's read the next letter to see what makes sense.

DIFFERENTIATING FOR EARLY LEARNERS WITH INDIVIDUAL NEEDS

Early Learners Who Excel With Support

At a young age, it is important to encourage children and be positive when helping them with alphabet letters. Early learners who might exhibit some reading deficiency should be treated with sensitivity. It is recommended that early intervention be a form of integrated approaches, such as teaching games and songs integrated with letter-sound relationships.

Early Learners Who Are Learning English

Reading wordless picture books or ABC picture books will help English language learners use picture representations with alphabet letters. Allow the child to pick books that are of interest. Some interesting ABC series books are being published by Sleeping Bear Press. One of my favorites that I bought for my children is *M is for Melody: A Music Alphabet* (Wargin, 2004). The illustrations are magnificent and will appeal to any young reader. Sleeping Bear Press publishes many other alphabet books for future reference.

Early Learners Who Excel

For learners who exhibit more advanced competency of the alphabet, encourage them to write letters of the alphabet and make their own ABC books by copying environmental print they select. To get started, read *The Important Book* by Margaret Wise Brown (1977). This book can be used to have a conversation about things that are important to the child. Make a book called *My Important ABCs Book*. Provide an opportunity to read the child's new book as a read-aloud.

TEACHING TIPS TO INCREASE HOME-SCHOOL CONNECTIONS

- Have access to lots of ABC books
- Encourage multisensory learning of ABCs
- Use environmental objects to practice letter-sound associations
- Use repetition, which is important to learning the alphabet
- Encourage use of music and games
- Use familiar names to practice the alphabet. Children enjoy learning about names.

LITERACY TREASURE CHEST

To help all learners who want to focus on developing the alphabetic principle, use Table 3.4 for literacy activities using ABC.

SUMMARY

Children love learning the letters and sounds of the alphabet, and it is probably one of the first milestones in their literate life. Understanding letter-sound associations is a first step to early reading. Early childhood educators and caregivers can enhance knowledge of the alphabetic principle by doing the following:

1. Use the natural environment with familiar words and sounds to begin helping children learn about the alphabet.

2. Use names, which are important for children. Children can begin letter-sound associations beginning with the letters in their name. See Table 3.5 for a summary of children's picture books with names in the titles.

3. Integrate alphabet knowledge development with daily activities.

4. Make available lots of print-rich material like ABC picture books.

5. Purchase mnemonic teaching materials from Zoo Phonics, a great resource, which can be located at www.zoophonics.com.

Table 3.4   Alphabet Books for Developing Beginning Reading Skills

ABC Picture Book Title	Integrated Literacy Activity
Extreme Animals Dictionary by Clint Twist (2004). New York: Scholastic.	Inspire children to make extreme animal hand puppets out of paper sacks and construction paper. While reading the book, children can hold up their puppet when appropriate.
K Is for Kissing a Cool Kangaroo by Giles Andreae and Guy Parker-Rees (2002). New York: Scholastic.	This is a fun book to help children understand that the alphabet letters have capital and small letters. Using magnetic alphabet letters, while reading this book children can sort the letters in ABC order as well as locate the small and capital letters.
Campbell Kids Alphabet Soup by Campbell Soup Co. (2004). New York: Abrams.	This is a great book to read on a cold day. Plan to have alphabet soup for lunch, and while reading this book, children can try to find and eat letters in the alphabet.
The Disappearing Alphabet by David Diaz (1997). New York: Harcourt Brace.	This book has interesting hidden alphabet letters on each page. Invite the children to do a picture walk together through the book first to see if they can find the alphabet letters. They will spend hours enjoying this book before you even get a chance to read it as a read-aloud. Once they have found the letters, have them write the letters on paper.
Ashanti to Zulu: African Traditions by Margaret Musgrove (1976). New York: Dial Books.	When learning about different cultures, this ABC book can be used to teach vocabulary about things that are different in other countries. It is recommended that this book be read a few pages at a time to allow for dialogic discussions.
America: A Patriotic Primer by Lynne Cheney (2004). New York: Scholastic.	This book is special because it talks about America and is a wonderful book to use during important days in our history such as the Fourth of July or President's Day. Before reading this book, write the A-Z letters of the alphabet on a chalkboard. Ask children to talk about the letters of the alphabet and have them think of words that begin with that letter that have to do with America. Invite children to talk first to encourage oral language development. This book is also a Caldecott Book and would be a great opportunity to talk about the Caldecott Medal.

Table 3.5   Children's Picture Books With Names in the Title

One Ted Falls Out of Bed by Julia Donaldson (2004). New York: Henry Holt.	This book is written by an author who wrote one of my very favorite books, *The Gruffalo.* The story is about a bear who falls. What is nice about this book are the rhyming words and beautiful illustrations.
Bebé Goes Shopping by Susan Middleton Elya (2006). New York: Harcourt.	Written using Spanish and English words, this book is perfect for English language learners.
Charlie Cook's Favorite Book by Julia Donaldson (2006). New York: Dial Books for Young Readers.	Charlie was a boy who loved books. The story takes Charlie on adventures that happen in his books. This book will help children think metacognitively.
Josephina Javeline by Susan Lowell (2005). Flagstaff, AR: Rising Moon.	A fictional story about three little javelinas. The names are in Spanish and the illustrations are scenes that you might see in the Southwest. Josephina has special talents that were described by her brothers as different. This book is great when talking about individuality.
Find Anthony Ant by Lorna and Graham Philpot (2006). New York: Sterling.	Anthony the Ant is trying to find his way through an underground ant maze. The book is fabulous for teaching children how to ask questions. The book also integrates counting. Use nonfiction books about bugs to enhance this book and increase comprehension.
Muti's Necklace by Louise Hawes (2006). New York: Houghton Mifflin.	The oldest story in the world is written on the front cover of this book, and it is said to be true. The illustrations are beautiful, and the plot will engage any reader who likes to hear stories.
Olivia's Opposites by Ian Falconer (2002). New York: Antheneum Books.	Described as an enchanting board book. Olivia, the very famous piglet, learns about things that are opposite and gets into a little trouble along the way.
There Once Was a Man Named Michael Finnegan by Mary Ann Hoberman (2001). New York: Little, Brown.	The author adapts this story from an old song, which is included in the book. Children will love the interactive form and the opportunity to sing about Michael Finnegan.
Sofia and the City by Karima Grant (2006). Honesdale, PA: Highlights.	Sofia is a young African American girl who has to deal with both parents working so they can live in the city. Sofia becomes upset because she thinks that no one notices her.
Russell and the Lost Treasure by Rob Scotton (2006). New York: Harper Collins.	The creative illustrations will engage any reader. The story about Russell begins with him finding a treasure map and continues with his search to find the treasure. It is a wonderful read-aloud with must-see pictures.
Augustus and His Smile by Catherine Rayner (2006). Intercourse, PA: Good Books.	Augustus is a big, beautiful tiger who lost his smile and is now sad. Augustus decides he will just have to find it. What is special about this book is the use of black in the illustrations as well as the unique way the author uses words.
Waiting for Gregory by Kimberly Willis Holt (2006). New York: Henry Holt.	This book is the winner of the National Book Award. It is a lovely story about a girl waiting for her brother to be born. While she is waiting, she asks special people in her life how her new brother will arrive. Grandfather says a stork will bring him.

Phonological Awareness

Giving Early Learners an Advantage When Learning to Read

by Kathryn Bauserman

Faced with an alphabetic script, the child's level of phonemic awareness on entering school may be the single most powerful determinant of the success she or he will experience in learning to read and of the likelihood that she or he will fail.

Dr. Marilyn Jager Adams (1995, p. 304)

Teaching introductory early childhood education courses at a community college, I frequently interject phonemic awareness activities into our class time. I do this because I want students to leave our program with an understanding of the importance of developing phonemic awareness as well as a repertoire of activities. Through phonemic awareness activities, children can develop a keener perception of the sounds of communication and become more attuned to the discrete sounds and patterns of language. Much like teaching math concepts by encouraging children to manipulate concrete materials over and over again to develop schema for shapes and number sense, phonemic awareness activities provide opportunities for children to manipulate sounds over and over again. College students enjoy using rhythm sticks to tap out syllables or rhymes. I hold up a picture and ask students to tap each sound or create a rhythm

S says /s/ like snowman /s/ /s/ /s/

T says /t/ like table /t/ /t/ /t/

Clapping hands, tapping feet, or jumping up and down also works. We also use it for vocabulary words.

T says /t/ like temporal /t/ /t/ /t/

P says /p/ like parietal /p/ /p/ /p/

For another game I divide the class in half and give students on each team a letter. Both teams have the same set of letters. I then say some sounds such as "ssss," "tttt," "pppp," and "oooo," and the students from both teams "walk quickly" to the front of the room and make a word ("pots," "stop," "tops," "spot"). Then teams are asked to take a sound away to make a word ("top"). The sound that leaves must say a sound, and the student on their team with that sound moves quickly to the front of the room to make another word. The leaving sound may also take one or two sounds away and call out another two or three sounds to make another word ("tempo"). A fast pace is the key to making it fun. Students are required to sound out the words as they make them. The first team to use all the sounds on their team wins.

The students enjoy manipulating the sounds. Through similar manipulations, children begin recognizing and organizing patterns: a key to intelligence, meaning making, and memory. These skills will be the foundation for later reading and writing.

Brenda Ragle, Early Childhood Professor at a Junior College

SOURCE: Vignette courtesy of Brenda Ragle.

The focus of this chapter is on phonological awareness and phonemic awareness, why these skills are important, and how to teach them well. Early Reading First (ERF) initiatives stress the need to teach preschool-age children phonological awareness and phonemic awareness skills and should be one of the primary goals for teaching preschool children according to the report of the National Reading Panel (NICHHD, 2000). As seen in the quote from Dr. Adams (1995, p. 304), phonemic awareness is a very high predictor of early reading success.

- What are phonological awareness and phonemic awareness?
- Why are they important in relationship to ERF teaching practices?
- What can teachers do to increase phonological awareness and phonemic awareness in emergent readers?
- How can I use the knowledge in this chapter to assist parents in guiding young children to acquire these skills?

Before looking at the research base, we need to understand the difference between phonemic awareness and the more general term phonological awareness. Phonological awareness refers to the ability to notice sounds in our language. This includes being aware of words, syllables, syllable parts (such as onsets and rimes), and individual sounds, called phonemes. (Onsets are the part of the syllable that comes before the vowel, and rimes are the part of the syllable that includes the vowel and anything that comes after it.) Phonological awareness also includes hearing rhyming words and alliteration (words with the same beginning sounds such as "Peter Piper picked a peck of pickled peppers"). Phonemic awareness has to do with hearing phonemes only. Phonemes are the smallest units of sound in spoken language, in other words, single sounds made by one or more letters. In print, sounds are represented by / /. For example, the grapheme (written letter) *t* makes the phonemic sound /t/. Sometimes a phoneme is spelled with more than one letter, such as *ea* in "eat," which says /e/.

Teachers often refer to phonemic awareness when they really mean phonological awareness because they are referring to sound units larger than phonemes. For example, when a teacher is talking about rhyming words ("cat" and "hat") or a syllable ("un-til"), the reference is to phonological awareness because the sound unit is larger than a phoneme. On the other hand, when the teacher is referring to a single sound (/d/), the reference is to phonemic awareness. In this chapter, both terms will be used: phonological awareness will always refer to the more encompassing awareness of all speech sounds (such as words, syllables, and onset and rimes), and phonemic awareness will be used only when referring to the sounds made by phonemes. Summarized below is the research base that supports the importance of phonological awareness and phonemic awareness as building blocks for early literacy educators.

RESEARCH THAT EARLY CHILDHOOD TEACHERS NEED TO KNOW ABOUT PHONOLOGICAL AWARENESS

The concept of phonemic awareness has been written about in literature for almost 100 years. In his seminal work *The Psychology and Pedagogy of Reading,* Huey (1908) spoke of the "mental isolation, for instance, of the unpronounceable sound t" (p. 214). He was referring to phonemic awareness even though he did not use that terminology. His conclusion was that beginning readers needed an awareness of phonemes in order to more easily learn to read. More recently, researchers have conducted research to determine the importance of phonological awareness and phonemic awareness abilities in emergent reading (Bauserman, 2003).

Adams (1995) wrote a summary of early research in this area and drew the following conclusions: (1) there was a strong relationship between phonological awareness and beginning reading achievement, (2) children's phonological awareness ability in preschool, kindergarten, and first grade was a powerful predictor of later reading achievement, (3) explicit training in phonemic awareness had a positive impact on reading and spelling skills, (4) phonemic awareness could be effectively trained prior to literacy instruction with a subsequent positive impact on reading ability, and (5) children trained in both phonemic awareness and letter names and sounds (in different activities, not simultaneously) did better in reading than children trained in only phonemic awareness. These conclusions illustrated the need for young children to develop phonological awareness skills.

More recently, the National Reading Panel (NRP) completed a comprehensive analysis (NICHHD, 2000) of scientifically based reading research on the components of reading, including phonological awareness and phonemic awareness. Its report included 57 research studies that met its standard for being scientifically based. Each study had an experimental design, meaning children were randomly assigned to a control group or to an experimental group. Students in the experimental groups were systematically taught phonological awareness and phonemic awareness skills. Each of the studies reported results using effect sizes. The more closely the reported effect size approaches 1.0, the more significant are the results of the study. The average effect size for the 57 studies was 0.53, a moderate level that precludes chance. Each study demonstrated that teaching preschool and kindergarten children phonological awareness and phonemic awareness improved their reading acquisition ability, including decoding words and comprehension.

The NRP drew the following conclusions: (1) phonological awareness, especially phonemic awareness, can be taught (Reitsma & Wesseling, 1998), (2) instruction in phonemic awareness helps all children learn to read, including children from low SES levels and English language learners (Barker & Torgesen, 1995), (3) phonemic awareness instruction helps all children learn to spell (O'Connor & Jenkins, 1995), and (4) the most effective phonemic awareness instruction is phoneme manipulation, the ability to exchange phoneme sounds in words (Murray, 1998). This research foundation provides broad support for teaching phonological awareness, especially phonemic awareness.

NEW RESEARCH-BASED PRACTICES THAT EARLY CHILDHOOD TEACHERS CAN USE

The NRP also reported the following implications for classroom instruction. Teachers need to be aware of these in order to implement effective instruction in the classroom.

1. Phonemic awareness acquisition is a means to an end—not the end. The desired result is helping children acquire skills for early reading acquisition. Children need to connect sounds to letters (alphabetic principle), so teaching letter names is also important.

2. Children differ in their phonemic awareness abilities, and some children will need more instruction than others.

3. Phonemic awareness instruction does not comprise a complete reading program. It is a foundation piece that helps children understand how the alphabetic principle works.

4. As with all effective teaching practices, exciting classroom activities to teach phonemic awareness and teacher enthusiasm for the instruction have a direct and positive impact on student learning.

5. The NRP warns: do not overgeneralize results from its analysis. Instructional methods from the 57 studies produced results that were not equally effective.

6. More is not better. The programs that contained approximately 20 hours of direct instruction in phonemic awareness were most effective.

7. There are no guarantees. Even though students from all SES levels, all ability levels, and English language learner students participated in the study, not all students will be guaranteed to achieve success in early reading acquisition.

Table 4.1 shows the developmental levels of phonological awareness. As can be seen, children begin with the phonological awareness of words, especially rhymes and alliterations. Then they progress to smaller units of sound (i.e., syllables). Words in sentences can be counted, then syllables in words can be counted. Furthermore, syllables can be broken into two parts, onsets and rimes. (See definitions in Table 4.1.) Finally, as children progress in their phonological awareness abilities, they develop an awareness of phonemes (i.e., phonemic awareness). There are many phonemic awareness skills: phoneme isolation, phoneme identity, phoneme oddity tasks, phoneme blending, phoneme segmenting, phoneme deletion, and finally phoneme manipulation. The phonemic awareness skills are also developmental in nature. Each level is a building block for the next level, and most children naturally follow the sequence suggested in the table. The range of age appropriateness is included in the table under Levels. It is to be noted that not all preschool children will be expected to master the highest developmental levels before ages five to six and some will master these higher level skills in kindergarten and beginning first grade.

One thing to remember about ERF is the importance of early instruction for children who might be at risk. Teachers who work with preschool-age children should understand the significance of phonological awareness and phonemic awareness and their critical roles in helping children learn to read. Because the levels are developmental, teachers need to begin instruction with rhymes and proceed through the table until their students reach the most difficult level—phoneme manipulation. Three lesson ideas are included here to guide teachers in how to teach phonological awareness and phonemic awareness skills. The sample lessons are for rhyme production, phoneme oddity tasks, and phoneme manipulation. The lessons are built around three popular children's books.

Table 4.1 Suggested Developmental Levels of Phonological Awareness, With Phonemic Awareness

Levels (appropriate ages)	Description/Features of Level	Instructional Activities & Interventions
Rhyme recognition (ages 2–5)	The child is able to recognize when two words rhyme, such as "cat" and "hat."	Read nursery rhymes. Read books with lots of rhyming words, such as Dr. Seuss books. Talk about the rhyming words.
Rhyme production (ages 2–5)	The child can respond to a rhyme prompt with an appropriate rhyming word; even nonsense rhymes are acceptable. When an adult asks, "What rhymes with cat?" the child might respond with "hat" or "wat." Any rhyming response is acceptable.	After reading a section of a rhyming book, model some rhyming words for the child, such as "cat," "hat," "vat," "fat." Ask the child to produce some more rhyming words.
Segmenting onsets and rimes (ages 3–5)	The child is able to break a one-syllable word into its onset and rime. (Onsets are the part of the syllable that comes before the vowel, and rimes are the part of the syllable that includes the vowel and anything that comes after it.) Example: Given "day," the child says /d/ /a/.	Pick some interesting one-syllable words from a book just read. Model how to separate the word into its onset and rime. Ask the child to repeat it after you. Repeat the modeling process until the child is able to segment the word into its onset and rime without modeling.
Blending onsets and rimes (ages 3–6)	Given an onset and rime combination, the child is able to blend them into the one syllable word they came from. (See description above.) Example: Given /d/ and /a/, the child says "day."	Pick some interesting one-syllable words from a book just read. Model how to blend the onset and rime into the word they came from. Ask the child to repeat it after you. Repeat the modeling process until the child is able to blend the onset and rime into the word without modeling.
Phoneme isolation (ages 4–6)	The child is able to isolate and say the beginning (or ending or middle/vowel sound). For example, when an adult asks, "What sound do you hear at the beginning of dog?" the child responds with "/d/" and/or the letter name d.	Choose interesting words from a favorite book and ask the child to tell you what sound is heard at the beginning. If the child is not able to isolate the phoneme, then model how it is done. Repeat the process until the child is able to perform independently. Progress to ending, then middle (vowel) sounds.
Phoneme identity (ages 4–6)	The child is able to identify by sound and/or name the common sound in a list of words, such as "big," "boy," and "bat." (They all begin with /b/ or b.)	Play this game with words from a favorite book or nursery rhyme: given a list of three words, the child can identify the common sound.
Phoneme oddity tasks (ages 4–6)	The child is able to determine if two words have the same beginning sounds or if their beginning sounds are different. After mastering beginning sounds, the child can hear if ending sounds and then middle (vowel) sounds are the same or different.	After reading any book, go back to a page and find two words with the same beginning sound. Ask the child if the words sound the same at the beginning. Then match one of the words with a word that does not begin with the same sound and repeat the question. Repeat this procedure for ending sounds, then middle (vowel) sounds.
Phoneme blending (ages 4–6)	Given three phonemes, the child is able to blend them into a word. For example: "What word do you get when you blend /b/ /a/ /k/?" The child responds with "bake."	Think of words to segment. Say the individual phonemes. Model how to blend the phonemes into a word. Ask the child to do it. Repeat until the child can blend phonemes independently.

Levels (appropriate ages)	Description/Features of Level	Instructional Activities & Interventions
Phoneme segmenting (ages 4–6)	Given a word with three phonemes, the child is able to segment the word into three phonemes. For example: "Tell me the three sounds you hear in 'kite.'" The child responds with /k/ /i/ /t/.	Think of a word with three phonemes. Model how to segment the three phonemes. Ask the child to do it. Repeat the process until the child can segment the phonemes independently.
Phoneme deletion (ages 5–7)	Given a word, the child can say the word without the beginning (or ending) phoneme. For example, "Say 'chair' without /ch/." The child responds with "air."	Using unique words from favorite books or family names, model how to say the word without its beginning (or ending) phoneme. Repeat the process until the child can delete phonemes independently.
Phoneme manipulation (ages 5–7)	The child is able to replace the beginning (ending or middle/vowel) phoneme. The adult asks: "What word would I make if I changed the /d/ in dog to /h/?" The child responds "hog." Repeat the process for ending and middle/vowel sounds.	Use the names of family and friends to play the Name Game. "Jim-Jim, Bo-Bim, Banana-nana Fo-Fim, Me, Mi, Mo-Mim. Jim"

SOURCE: Levels were synthesized from the National Reading Panel Report (National Institute of Child Health and Human Development, 2000) and Adams, 1995.

Lessons for Early Childhood Teachers to Encourage Phonological Awareness

Rhyme Production

Key book: *The Snowy Day* by Ezra Jack Keats (1962)

An Early Childhood Teacher Might Say: (After reading the book) "I love this book, don't you? The young boy in the story has some great adventures. Tell me the name of the young boy who played in the snow. [Children respond with "Peter."] Where did Peter have his great adventures? [Children respond with "snow."] I can think of some words that rhyme with snow. Remember, rhymes sound like the end of the word, but they have a different sound at the beginning. For example: snow-bow. They both say "–ow," but they have different sounds at the beginning. Can you help me think of some words that rhyme with snow?"

The Teacher May Want to Have Students: The teacher will have students provide rhyming words for snow. The teacher writes all suggestions on chart paper. She points out that the words all end with "–ow" so that students can visually see the similarities, even if they don't know the letters. Nonsense words are acceptable responses.

(Continued)

(Continued)

Lesson Could Be Assessed By: The teacher can assess the effectiveness of the lesson by asking children to repeat the process with some of the other words from the story, like sun. Can they think of rhymes without teacher modeling? Can each child provide a rhyme?

Phoneme Oddity Tasks

Key book: *Abuela's Big Bed* by Ina Cumpiano (1995)

An Early Childhood Teacher Might Say: (After reading the book) "I think this book is great. There are some fun words in this story. Let me reread a page from the story, and you remember a word that I read that you like. [Teacher reads a page.] Tell me a word that you like from the page I just read. [Child gives response such as 'fuss.'] Listen to the beginning sound of 'fuss.' Does it sound the same as the beginning sound of 'funny? Fuss, funny. [Children say, 'Yes.'] Does it sound the same as the beginning of the sound of 'bed'? Fuss, bed. [Children say, 'No.']" Repeat the process with some other examples.

The Teacher May Want to Have Students: The teacher will have students respond to her oddity task questions with thumbs up if the words sound the same, thumbs down if they are different.

Lesson Could Be Assessed By: The teacher can assess the effectiveness of the lesson by monitoring thumbs up/thumbs down responses. Children who consistently have incorrect responses may need some more individual or small group help with the concept.

Phoneme Manipulation

Key book: *Mouse Count* by Ellen Stoll Walsh (1991)

An Early Childhood Teacher Might Say: (After reading the book) "I like to read this book, don't you? There are some great animal characters in this book. Tell me the name of the animal that was very hungry. [Children respond with 'snake.'] Tell me the name of the animals that tricked the snake. [Children respond with 'mice.'] Let's sing the Name Game for these two names."

The Teacher May Want to Have Students: The teacher will have the students sing the Name Game song for snake and mice. "Snake, snake, Bo-bake, banana-nana fo-fake, me, mi, mo-make. Snake." Repeat the song with mice.

Lesson Could Be Assessed By: The teacher can assess the effectiveness of the lesson by asking children to repeat one of the "new" names (for snake or mice) they sang in the song. Also, did the children enjoy singing the song?

EARLY READING FIRST ASSESSMENT
TOOLS FOR PHONEMIC AWARENESS

Assessment Name: Dynamic Indicators of Basic Early Literacy Skills (DIBELS)

Subtests: ISF: Initial Sound Fluency, LNF: Letter Naming Fluency, PSF: Phoneme Segmentation Fluency

Assessment Goals:

ISF: To identify a child's ability to match the given beginning sound to the correct picture in a set of four; given to children from preschool through mid-kindergarten

LNF: To identify a child's ability to name a random collection of lower- and upper-case alphabet letters; given to children from beginning kindergarten through beginning first grade

PSF: To identify a child's ability to segment the sounds heard in words with three or four phonemes; given to children from the end of kindergarten through the end of first grade

How to Administer: These assessments are easy to administer. They are administered individually in a one-minute time frame. The DIBELS Web site provides complete administration instructions and video clips of a sample administration. DIBELS is also available in Spanish.

SOURCE: Created by University of Oregon; free downloads available on the Web site: www.dibels.uoregon.edu/

Assessment Name: Yopp-Singer Phonemic Segmentation Assessment

Assessment Goal: This instrument is designed to assess a child's ability to segment phonemes.

How to Administer: This assessment is individually administered. There are only 22 items on this oral assessment. Scripted directions are provided for the examiner's benefit. The test is not timed. It is appropriate to give to preschool children through early elementary school. It can be given in conjunction with the Lipson & Wixson Phonemic Blending Assessment (see below).

SOURCE: Yopp, 1955.

Assessment Name: Lipson & Wixson Phonemic Blending Assessment

Assessment Goal: This instrument is for assessing a child's ability to blend phonemes.

How to Administer: The 10-item assessment is untimed. Scripted directions are provided for the examiner's benefit. It is appropriate to give to preschool children through early elementary school. It is to be given in conjunction with the Yopp-Singer Phonemic Segmentation Assessment (see above).

SOURCE: Lipson & Wixson, 2003.

DIFFERENTIATING FOR EARLY LEARNERS WITH INDIVIDUAL NEEDS

Early Learners Who Excel With Support

At a very young age, children begin to explore the sounds of our language, even before they learn to talk well. Early childhood teachers need to encourage language play by modeling it and encouraging children to explore making sounds with their mouths and tongues. These explorations are prerequisites for building phonological awareness and phonemic awareness. Early learners who might be struggling with language production and exploration might need more encouragement and modeling by adults. The various levels of phonological awareness from Table 4.1. can be used as a guide. The levels listed are generally developmental, meaning children are able to recognize rhymes before producing rhymes, and so on. Teachers also need to provide positive reinforcement to encourage early learners who can excel with support.

Early Learners Who Are Learning English

As schools become more global, early childhood educators need to be aware of the changing cultures in their classrooms. Not all children may have English as their first language. Teachers need to be informed about ways they can help their students develop oral language, in general, and phonological awareness, specifically. English language learners benefit from many social opportunities to learn language from their peers, and classroom teachers can help create such opportunities. Fortunately, most phonemes cross all languages, so teachers are not teaching new sounds, just the order in which the sounds are connected. Early learners who are learning English are also much attuned to sounds in their second language and are already naturally making comparisons to their native language.

Early Learners Who Excel

Early childhood educators can challenge students who excel by moving them along the suggested developmental levels of phonological awareness from Table 4.1. As teachers informally assess the mastery of phonological awareness levels, they can continually challenge their exceptional students with activities at the next level of phonological awareness. Advancing early learners who excel faster than their peers will get them ready to read just that much sooner.

TEACHING TIPS THAT INCREASE HOME-SCHOOL CONNECTIONS

- Parent/Guardian Visitation Night: Introduce phonological awareness and explain its importance in the emergent reading process. Then model some of the phonological awareness activities that you are currently doing in your classroom so that parents can understand how to do similar activities at home. Tell parents you will include an activity each week in the newsletter.

- Parent Newsletter: Each week explain one of the levels of phonological awareness (from Table 4.1) that you are currently working on in your classroom. Since your class may work on the same level for several weeks, share a different activity each week for parents to do at home to practice the skill with their child.

LITERACY TREASURE CHEST

In order to help all learners develop phonological awareness skills, Table 4.2 lists some excellent books that are recommended for educators to use in the read-aloud format. The same book can be read multiple times with a different emphasis each time. Many phonological awareness skills can be taught from the same book.

SUMMARY

Phonological awareness skills, especially phonemic awareness skills, are the single best predictor of successful early reading acquisition. In order for children to have advantages in developing reading skills, they must master many phonological awareness skills in their early years. Early childhood educators can effectively develop phonological awareness skills in their early learners, thus increasing the likelihood of more efficient reading acquisition during the early years of schooling. Here is a summary of what you have learned in this chapter that you can use in your classroom:

1. Phonological awareness, especially phonemic awareness, is very important for early reading success.

2. There are 11 developmental levels of phonological awareness.

3. Children in your classroom will have a large range of phonological awareness abilities.

4. Phonological awareness can be taught to all students.

5. Teachers can use words from favorite books to create exciting phonological awareness activities.

Table 4.2 Books That Can Be Used to Teach Phonological Awareness Skills

Level of Phonological Awareness (from Table 4.1)	Recommended Books for Early Childhood Educators to Read Aloud
Rhyme recognition These books have lots of rhyming words for children to recognize.	*Brown Bear, Brown Bear, What Do You See?* by Bill Martin Jr. (1983). New York: Holt, Rinehart, & Winston. *The Cat in the Hat* by Dr. Seuss (1957). Boston: Houghton Mifflin. Traditional nursery rhymes
Rhyme production Children can produce many rhymes using words in these books.	*The Nose Book* by Dr. Seuss (1970). New York: Random House. *The Foot Book* by Dr. Seuss (1968). New York: Random House. There are many other rhyming books by Dr. Seuss.
Segmenting onsets and rimes There are lots of great words in these books to segment into onsets and rimes.	*Five Little Monkeys Jumping on the Bed* by Eileen Christelow (1989). New York: Clarion Books. *Five Little Monkeys Sitting in a Tree* by Eileen Christelow (1991). New York: Clarion Books. *Five Little Monkeys Wash the Car* by Eileen Christelow (2000). New York: Clarion Books.
Blending onsets and rimes There are lots of great words in these books to use for blending onsets and rimes.	*Five Little Monkeys With Nothing to Do* by Eileen Christelow (1996). New York: Clarion Books. *Don't Wake up Mama! Another Five Little Monkeys Story* by Eileen Christelow (1992). New York: Clarion Books. *Five Little Monkeys Play Hide-and-Seek* by Eileen Christelow (2004). New York: Clarion Books.
Phoneme isolation These books have a huge variety of words for phoneme isolation activities.	*If You Give a Mouse a Cookie* by Laura Numeroff (1985). New York: Harper & Row. *If You Take a Mouse to School* by Laura Numeroff (2000). New York: Laura Geringer Book. *If You Take a Mouse to the Movies* by Laura Numeroff (2000). New York: Laura Geringer Book.
Phoneme identity These alphabet books are full of great words for phoneme identity activities.	*Apples, Alligators and also Alphabets* by Odette & Bruce Johnson (1990). New York: Scholastic. *Ashanti to Zulu: African Traditions* by Margaret Musgrove (1976). New York: Dial Books. *K is for Kwanzaa: A Kwanzaa Alphabet Book* by Juwanda G. Ford (1997). New York: Scholastic.
Phoneme oddity tasks Eric Carle books have some great words to use for oddity tasks.	*The Very Hungry Caterpillar* by Eric Carle (1987). New York: Philomel Books. *The Grouchy Ladybug* by Eric Carle (1999). New York: HarperFestival. *The Very Lonely Firefly* by Eric Carle (1995). New York: Philomel Books.
Phoneme blending Teachers and children can select some good one-syllable words for blending phonemes.	*There Was an Old Lady Who Swallowed a Fly* by Simms Taback (1997). New York: Viking. *There Was an Old Lady Who Swallowed a Bat* by Lucille Colandro (2002). New York: Scholastic. There are many other books in this series.
Phoneme segmenting Some excellent one-syllable words can be selected for segmenting phonemes.	*Moonbear's Pet* by Frank Asch (1997). New York: Simon & Schuster Books for Young Readers. *Moonbear's Dream* by Frank Asch (1999). New York: Simon & Schuster Books for Young Readers. *Moonbear's Skyfire* by Frank Asch (1999). New York: Aladdin.
Phoneme deletion Most words from these books can be used to delete beginning phonemes.	*The Butter Battle Book* by Dr. Seuss (1984). New York: Random House. *Horton Hears a Who* by Dr. Seuss (1954). New York: Random House. *Yertle the Turtle* by Dr. Seuss (1958). New York: Random House.
Phoneme manipulation Lots of words in the Frog and Toad books can be used for phoneme manipulation.	*Frog and Toad All Year* by Arnold Lobel (1976). New York: Scholastic. *Days With Frog and Toad* by Arnold Lobel (1979). New York: Scholastic. *Frog and Toad Together* by Arnold Lobel (1971). New York: Harper & Row.

5

Print Awareness

by Cynthia A. Lassonde

Words, once they are printed, have a life of their own.

Carol Burnett

Lassonde Farm Nursery School was the name of the preschool I owned and operated. The program the teachers and I offered focused on language-experience literacy activities in which we took real-life farm experiences and made them opportunities to learn about what it meant to be a reader and writer. Each week there was a farm focus. One week in the spring we watched a farmer shear a sheep. Other weeks we saw how a farrier shod a horse, we picked apples from our orchard, and we snaked through a hayfield when the hay was almost taller than the children. We took these experiences back into the classroom and read about them, drew and wrote about them, and followed the words on a chart while we sang about them. Developmentally these students were just beginning to understand that the words I pointed to on the chart and in the books we shared had meaning. By repeatedly seeing the word "horse," they were starting to recognize that the shapes of the letters were consistent each time they saw them and that the word had a particular meaning. Our goal for these preschoolers was to help them develop their print awareness so they could blossom as emergent readers preparing to enter kindergarten.

Cynthia A. Lassonde

- What is print awareness in relation to Early Reading First (ERF) teaching practices?
- What can teachers do to increase print awareness in emergent readers?
- How can I use the knowledge in this chapter to assist families in guiding young children?

In this chapter, we focus on the development and promotion of print awareness in emergent readers. Print awareness—an emergent reader's earliest literacy skill—has been found to correlate positively with reading skills and abilities in the early grades (Christie, Enz, & Vukelich, 2007). Like the children who attended Lassonde Farm Nursery School, children who understand concepts of print, book concepts, and know some basic sight words—the components of print awareness—will be better achievers in reading than those who are not comfortable with these notions. Children who begin school without print awareness may be at risk for reading difficulty (Clay, 1993).

The goals of the ERF program include preparing young children, particularly those from low-income families, to enter kindergarten with a foundation in print awareness and other reading skills to benefit from formal school instruction (U.S. Department of Education, 2004). The program aims to demonstrate literacy activities in print awareness that are based on scientific research in reading. Key understandings upon which early childhood practices should be based are described next.

RESEARCH THAT EARLY CHILDHOOD TEACHERS NEED TO KNOW ABOUT PRINT AWARENESS

Current research in reading and early childhood development provides insight about print awareness at the emergent level. To begin, let's take a look at how educators and researchers are defining print awareness. As described by current researchers and educators in the early childhood field (McGee & Richgels, 2004; Morrow & Gambrell, 2004; Schickedanz & Casbergue, 2004; Strickland & Schickedanz, 2004), there are several components involved. A child is developing print awareness when he or she begins to do the following:

- Understand that the purpose of written language is to communicate; that those marks on the page hold some kind of meaning (concept of print)
- Notice environmental print
- Understand that letters have names and distinct shapes and form words (concept of letter)
- Distinguish between print and pictures, letters and words, words and the spaces between them (concept of word)
- Track print and recognize print has directionality—top to bottom, left to right in the English language (concept of print)
- Identify the parts of a book and their purposes (book concepts)
- Recognize and know the purpose for punctuation (concept of punctuation)

- Recognize some sight words
- Show signs of recognizing print symbols when drawing that lead to writing

Christie et al. (2006) describe three components of print awareness. They are, as previously listed, concepts of print, which include concepts of letter, word, sentence, and punctuation; book concepts; and sight words. Concepts of print are the functions or practical uses of written language, the structure of words and sentences, and the conventions of print (Vukelich, Christie, & Enz, 2007). Book concepts refer to knowing the jargon used to identify the parts of a book, such as title, author, illustrator, title page; the purpose for each part; as well as where to begin reading, how to hold a book, and where to start reading the story. There are 24 concepts about print and book concepts ranging from orientation of book and directionality to punctuation and first-and-last letter concepts (Clay, 1993).

Sight words are also sometimes listed in reading literature as one of the components of print awareness (Christie et al., 2006). Typically, sight words are recognized immediately as a whole rather than being decoded by the reader. Words that are phonetically irregular often are taught as sight words along with words considered important for emergent readers to learn before they have decoding skills because they appear frequently in beginning readers (Harris & Hodges, 1995). The Dolch sight word list is readily available online. One site where it may be found is literacyconnections.com/Dolch1.html.

Now that we have a good understanding of how the literature distinguishes all the terms related to print awareness, let's consider the role of the family—the child's first reading teacher—in its development. Family literacy plays a very important role in the child's development of emergent print awareness because typically the child learns first about the purposes of reading and writing, how to handle a book, and the meaning behind environmental print by interacting with family and modeling family behaviors. Therefore, to address the goals of ERF, the role of preparing children at risk for literacy delays begins with family literacy or how family members read and write together and independently (Taylor, 1983) and the family's "funds of knowledge" (Moll & Greenberg, 1990), or what the family contributes to a child's wealth of literacy understandings (Moll & Greenberg, 1990).

Frequently, a child's first understandings about print come when the child recognizes that a certain logo on a cereal box or sign along the road has consistent meaning. Environmental print can have a high impact as a young child's first exposure to the code system of written symbols (Prior & Gerard, 2004). Early readers construct a "cognitive anchor" to map sounds and meanings onto written codes. Environmental print, such as a stop sign, can be this anchor for a child to make the connection between print and meaning when he or she recognizes that every time the car comes to this sign, the car stops. Adult instruction is key to securing this anchor when it draws attention to letters and sounds in environmental print words—the /s/ in "stop"—and helps the child transfer this new information to other texts, especially those without accompanying graphics, such as the color and shape of the stop sign.

Print awareness does not just happen. It must be modeled, talked about, and explicitly taught. Research indicates these concepts are best taught within the context of authentic reading activities, such as when interactively reading with children (Justice & Ezell, 2002). In the next section, we look at several practices that support print awareness and are based on scientific reading research.

NEW RESEARCH-BASED PRACTICES THAT EARLY CHILDHOOD TEACHERS CAN USE

In early childhood education, promoting school success involves integrating physical, cognitive, and social areas of development (Blair, 2002). The security and comfort of dependable teacher-student relationships help a child's overall development thrive. The following are suggested practices that integrate physical, cognitive, and social development and support positive teacher-student relationships in ways that promote print awareness. Three practices will be discussed: read-alouds, writing with children, and dramatic-play-with-print centers.

Read-Alouds

Reading aloud to children has multiple benefits and advantages to promote emergent literacy. Time spent reading to children should be not only a learning experience as new concepts and vocabulary are introduced, but it should be a social time in which readers interact with the book through enriching and enjoyable conversations about the story and related connections. In Chapter 2 an outline of how to use read-alouds to model and stimulate oral language was described. The read-aloud is also an excellent way to model and promote understanding of the three components of print awareness, that is, concept of print, book concepts, and sight words. In an effective read-aloud, children will learn that print carries meaning, repeated words are consistently read the same way, the title helps the reader predict what the book will be about, and there is a difference between written and oral language (Morrow & Gambrell, 2000). To develop print awareness, practice the following strategies before, during, and after reading.

Before Reading Aloud:
- Talk about how you position a book right side up to read it
- Demonstrate the front and the back covers of the book and their purposes
- Point to the title and talk with the child about how the title helps us predict what the book will be about
- Have the child talk about the picture on the front cover and predict from the picture what the story might be about

- Read the author's and illustrator's names and ask the child what their roles are
- Select several vocabulary words (sight words, high-frequency words, or unfamiliar words) from the story. Discuss them and write them on a card (Reading Rockets, 2006)

During the Read-Aloud:

- Track the words with your finger as you read, demonstrating directionality (top to bottom, left to right for English language)
- Encourage child to look for the vocabulary words you selected and discussed before reading and to predict what will happen next in the story (Reading Rockets, 2006)
- Explain that you are reading the words

After Reading Aloud:

- Discuss the child's predictions of what the book would be about by using the cover picture and title.
- Have the child talk about how you told the story by reading the print.
- Have the child talk about the concepts of print, word, letter, sentence, and punctuation ideas that emerged from the particular story you shared
- Ask if there were any words that were repeated throughout the book and if the child can find them in the print

Writing With Children

Young children quickly discover that print is used to get things done. It is functional. A child's own writing is one of the most relevant forms of print for him or her (Soderman, Gregory, & McCarty, 2005).

We now view even early scribbling as a stage in the development of emergent writing skills. Sulzby (1990) describes writing stages in which children progress from drawing and scribbling to forming letter-like shapes and finally letters before they begin to make phonetic connections between letters and sounds, use invented spelling, and move toward conventional spelling. While generally children move forward through the stages, they also move back and forth across the stages when composing texts and may even combine stages within one piece of writing (Sulzby, 1992). During the emergent stages of writing, children develop small-muscle and eye-hand coordination to manipulate writing tools as they learn the features and purposes of written language through socialization.

Concepts of print are evident when a child draws or scribbles shapes and lines and asks, "What does that say?" Print awareness is developed further through writing experiences when the child is taught to write and form the conventional shapes of the letters. Through writing experiences, the child develops an understanding of the difference between a letter and a word. Having a child find all the *d*'s on a page of a book and then writing *d*'s will help reinforce the concept.

The idea of using a child's name as an anchor for learning about concepts of letters and words has been proven as an effective strategy. Bell and Jarvis (2002) found that when children's names are used as a familiar text, they are confident in taking what they know about their name to build new understandings about other words and letters. Examples of concepts and practices that expand on what children know about their name to develop print awareness include the following:

- Teaching directionality concepts: the letters in the child's name are written from left to right as are letters in other words; the first letter the child writes when writing his or her name is the first sound heard when saying the name. Stretching the child's name by saying it slowly and emphasizing sounds heard at the beginning, middle, and ending while writing the name reinforces letter-sound connections and directionality

- Letter recognition and writing: relate the letters and sounds from a child's name to new words the child wants to write (e.g., "That word starts with the same letter your name starts with. What is that letter?")

- Noting visual characteristics of letters: after the child writes his or her name, have the child write all the letters in the name that have circles or curves (e.g., *o, a, e*), short sticks (e.g., *m, n*), long sticks (e.g., *h, 1*), hills (e.g., *m, n*), and tails (e.g., *g, j*). Apply this to letters in other words

Dramatic-Play-With-Print Centers

Preschool and kindergarten classrooms often include housekeeping or dress-up areas in which children engage in dramatic pretend play. Dramatic-play-with-print centers are strategically planned dramatic play centers that promote engagement in themed play that offers opportunities for students to read and write (Neuman & Roskos, 1990). Emergent readers and writers may scribble doctor prescriptions on a pad; "mommies" and "daddies" may write shopping lists or read cereal boxes. These centers, when carefully planned and stocked with print props, encourage the development of print awareness by situating a context with which children are familiar. Children who have been to a grocery store or beauty salon/barbershop have observed functions of print in those environments and will play at mimicking what people do in these settings.

Teachers or family members may further enhance the play experience by playing with the children to model more complex ways in which print is used in these settings (Morrow & Rand, 1991). For example, a teacher playing with children in a bookstore center may say, "We don't have that book in our store right now, but let me write down the name of it and I can order it for you." The teacher may also capitalize on a child's idea to sort canned food on the shelf of a grocery store center by lining cans up with like letters together (i.e., putting the peas and pears on the shelf together).

**EARLY READING FIRST ASSESSMENT
TOOLS FOR PRINT AWARENESS**

Assessment Name: The Observation Survey, Part II: Concept About Print Test

Assessment Goal: To check what the emergent reader has learned about the way language is printed.

How to Administer: This assessment takes 5 to 10 minutes. The child is given a copy of two books (*Sand* and *Stones* by Clay, 1972, 1979). A script is provided for the assessor of what to say. In the context of reading the text to the child, a conversation occurs that helps the assessor observe and record the child's responses to prompts about 24 concepts of print, letter, word, punctuation, and book concepts. The assessment is easily scored using a table of Stanine scores. Instructions for interpreting results are also provided.

SOURCE: Clay (1972, 1979, 1993).

Assessment Name: Phonological Awareness Literacy Screening PreK (PALS-PreK)

Note: Use the Print and Word Awareness and Word Recognition sections (for beginning sight word recognition).

Assessment Goal: To assess a battery of emergent reading skills, including name writing, alphabet recognition, letter sounds, print awareness, and rhyme awareness.

How to Administer: Materials, scoring, benchmarks, and administration guide, student booklets, and script available in screening packet. Both sections take approximately 15 minutes to administer.

SOURCE: Invernizzi, Sullivan, Meier, & Swank (2004).

DIFFERENTIATING FOR LEARNERS WITH INDIVIDUAL NEEDS

Early Learners Who Excel With Support

Confusions about the seemingly arbitrary conventions of our written language tend to persist and remain baffling for some students who require reading support (Clay, 1993). When print cues are embedded in book-reading sessions, research indicates at-risk readers showed gains on print awareness measures (Justice & Ezell, 2002). Also, Cambourne (2001) tells us that children who are exposed to demonstrations of how to read and write sometimes do not engage with them or do not think they are capable of learning to read or write. Therefore, the demonstrations are not effective. This would indicate that when teaching print awareness skills, we must not only thoroughly and accurately demonstrate them but must find ways to involve and motivate students to want to participate and learn.

Early Learners Who Are Learning English

Second-language learners readily transfer what they know about reading and writing from their first language to their second language because they have learned what they know in the native language that they understand (Garcia, 1994). Students do not have to start from the beginning of reading when learning a new language. They should be encouraged to transfer and use what they know from prior experiences with print. If a child has been read to and has been part of authentic literacy events with embedded purposes for reading and writing in the home environment, the child is becoming literate. First-language literates have been documented as being able to transfer literacy skills to their second language, while first-language illiterates were markedly disadvantaged (Rodriguez, 2001). Therefore, early childhood teachers who recognize a second-language learner's literacy development in the first language will view the student's prior experiences as assets upon which to build more advanced skills in print awareness.

Rodriguez (2001) recommends that as teachers of second-language learners, we look for the cognates or similarities that exist in literacy events of both languages and explicitly discuss with the child which similarities exist and transfer from the first to the second language and which skills contrast from one language to the next. For example, there are many similarities in print awareness between English and Spanish. However, in other languages, such as Chinese, there will be many more differences, such as directionality of print and the use of alphabetic letters. In print awareness, some cognates, such as the idea that written language carries meaning, are universal, however.

In light of the research, the early childhood teacher should spend time becoming familiar with the structure of the first languages of children in their class. Talk with the families to determine what the child's experiences with print have been at home to date. Sit with the child to observe how a book is handled. If possible, watch an interaction between the adult family member and the child over the reading of a book. Observe whether and, if so, how the child engages, takes note of the pictures and print, talks about the book, and tries to involve the adult. Above all, demonstrate to the family and to the child that the child's first language and prior literacy experiences with print are valuable and respected.

Let's revisit Cambourne's (2001) proposal in a previous section that children must engage in literacy events in order for the student to learn and to be motivated to read. Consider the second-language learner sitting and listening to an early childhood teacher read a book the child does not comprehend. Readers must be familiar with at least 95% of the vocabulary in a text to understand the story (Carrell & Grabe, 2002). Will children participate in the story if they cannot understand it? The potential for the student to become highly involved is unlikely. Therefore, as teachers we must remember to choose books with limited vocabulary and illustrations that clearly depict the story line at first to hook the child into engaging in the process of reading a book. Then, as the child becomes more proficient, move on to more difficult books. This does not mean the whole class has to be read only books the second-language learner can comprehend, but that books should be selected to meet the needs of diverse reading abilities. Also, time should be scheduled regularly to work in small groups of mixed-level students so there are opportunities to focus on more individual needs of students while offering peer models of more advanced reading.

Early Learners Who Excel

When a child is already demonstrating knowledge and ability to apply emergent levels of print awareness, introducing the child to complex texts will provide opportunities to learn types of print awareness typically not included in beginning readers. For example, book concepts such as chapters, chapter titles, and captions are a few terms that may be introduced by exploring more advanced books. At Lassonde Farm Nursery School, I often brought in reference books to share pictures and information on different kinds of horses or trees. These books led to discussions of how diagrams were labeled, how to use a table of contents or index, and the purpose of these kinds of books.

TEACHING TIPS THAT INCREASE HOME-SCHOOL CONNECTIONS

Perhaps more than in any other stage of early reading, families are so important in helping children gain awareness of print, for it is through their daily observations and interactions with the adults in their lives that children will learn from a young age the magic that happens from the squiggly lines on a page of paper. Working with families and accessing the knowledge children bring to a formal learning environment is crucial to helping prepare young emergent readers. Early childhood teachers should help to build upon families' "funds of knowledge" (Moll & Greenberg, 1990) to help them support their children's print awareness abilities. This is possible by encouraging and teaching families how to do the following:

- Point out and talk about concepts of print, book concepts, and sight words as they read aloud with their child on a regular basis. Embed terms, such as title, author, period, question mark, letter, word, beginning, end, in their talk about books during authentic literacy events.
- Have materials around the house so the child can draw and write during play activities. Drawing and scribbling lead to the use of letters and words to help communicate pretend messages as they develop print awareness. Schickedanz and Casbergue (2004) recommend that to make the literacy event complete and effective, families offer physical and social support for children's writing by providing not only an appropriate physical context (e.g., a kitchen table) and motivating materials, but also a purpose for the activity and adult involvement to extend growth and thinking.
- Demonstrate authentic purposes for reading and writing and invite the child to "help you" read or write to figure something out. Let your child "catch" you reading or writing for real purposes, including enjoyment.
- Recognize and praise your child's first attempts at reading and writing.

LITERACY TREASURE CHEST

Following is a list of early predictable books that I have used in my work with emergent readers at my nursery school and with my own children. Predictable books invite children to join in on the story based on the ease of guessing what comes next. The child gets swept up in the flow and rhythm of the book due to a familiar sequence, pattern, repetition, rhyming scheme, or some other element of predictability (Christie et al., 2007).

I have selected these particular books not only because children and I have enjoyed them but because they encourage children to read along based on their repetition and simplistic phrasing. With few words on a page, it is easy for the reader—adult or child—to clearly track each word while reading with a pointer or finger. Also, these books are filled with high-frequency sight words that are repeated over and over again. All of these characteristics will help the child understand the concept of print and learn sight word vocabulary, especially when used in an effective read-aloud in which the reader and child talk about the underlying skills and concepts that take place during the reading process. Enjoy!

Asch, F. (1984). *Just Like Daddy.* New York: Simon & Schuster Children's.

Archambault, J., & Martin, B. (1989). *Chicka Chicka Boom Boom!* New York: Simon & Schuster.

Brown, R. (1992). *A Dark, Dark Tale.* New York: Puffin Books.

Carle, E. (1994). *The Very Hungry Caterpillar.* New York: Penguin Young Readers Group.

Christelow, E. (1998). *Five Little Monkeys Jumping on the Bed.* Boston: Houghton Mifflin.

Dunbar, J. (1992). *Four Fierce Kittens.* New York: Scholastic.

Dunphy, M. (1997). *Here Is the Tropical Rain Forest.* McHenry, IL: Sagebrush Education Resources.

Eastman, P. (1960). *Are You My Mother?* New York: Random House.

Galdone, P. (1983). *The Gingerbread Boy.* Boston: Houghton Mifflin.

Galdone, P. (1985). *The Little Red Hen.* Boston: Houghton Mifflin.

Galdone, P. (1991). *Little Tuppen: An Old Tale.* Boston: Houghton Mifflin.

Gunson, C. (1996). *Over on the Farm.* New York: Corgi Children's Books.

Hawkins, C., & Hawkins, J. (1991). *I Know an Old Lady Who Swallowed a Fly.* London, England: Egmont Children's Books.

Hennessy, B. (1992). *Jake Baked the Cake.* New York: Penguin Young Readers Group.

Kovalski, M. (1990). *The Wheels on the Bus.* Tonawanda, NY: Kids Can Press.

Krauss, R. (1989). *The Carrot Seed.* New York: HarperCollins.

London, J. (2002). *Wiggle Waggle.* Orlando, FL: Harcourt.

MacDonald, M. R. (2007). *Old Woman and Her Pig: An Appalachian Folktale.* New York: HarperCollins.

Martin, B. (1996). *Brown Bear, Brown Bear, What Do You See?* New York: Henry Holt.

Martin, B. (1997). *Polar Bear, Polar Bear, What Do You Hear?* New York: Henry Holt.

Most, B. (1984). *If the Dinosaurs Came Back.* Orlando, FL: Harcourt.

Numeroff, L. (1985). *If You Give a Mouse a Cookie.* New York: HarperCollins.

Peek, M. (1998). *Mary Wore Her Red Dress.* Boston: Houghton Mifflin.

Polacco, P. (1997). *In Enzo's Splendid Gardens.* New York: Penguin Young Readers Group.

Sendak, M. E. (1991). *Pierre, A Cautionary Tale.* New York: HarperCollins.

West, C. (1996). *"Buzz, Buzz, Buzz," Went Bumblebee.* Cambridge, MA: Candlewick Press.

West, J. (2000). *Have You Got My Purr?* New York: Dutton Children's Books.

Williams, S. (1996). *I Went Walking.* Orlando, FL: Harcourt Children's Books.

6

Designing Early
Literacy Classrooms
of Excellence

I touch the future. I teach.

Christa McAuliffe

Before I went to kindergarten, my mother used to take me to the library to listen to the librarian read stories once a week. What was nice about the library were all the books I had access to while I was there. I also enjoyed the many different games we would play that went along with the books she read to us. Since early childhood centers were not as well supported when I was growing up, my vision of a center of excellence would be an environment with lots of books for children to read and lots of opportunities for integrated play activities to go along with the stories.

Susan E. Israel

Thus far, you have learned about the key components of Early Reading First (ERF). Now that you have established your background knowledge, you will be well prepared to establish your goals to design early literacy classrooms of excellence. The U.S. Department of Education recommends that when creating centers or classrooms of excellence, the focus should be placed on improving the quality of the environment at the center, as well as the literacy curriculum. This chapter responds to the goals of ERF by describing early childhood environments that will allow children to enter kindergarten with the prerequisites of language, cognitive, and early reading and writing skills in order to benefit from early reading instruction (U.S. Department of Education, 2004). In this chapter, the following questions are answered:

- What do early literacy environments of excellence look like?
- What resources do I need to maintain a center of excellence?
- How can teachers maintain an environment of educational excellence while at the same time integrating the key components of ERF in the literacy curriculum?
- What goals should we have to establish a center of excellence?
- What do I need to know to apply for funding?

RESEARCH THAT EARLY CHILDHOOD TEACHERS NEED TO KNOW ABOUT CREATING CENTERS OF EXCELLENCE

The U.S. Department of Education supports the development of early childhood centers of excellence by providing ERF grants to eligible schools with an emphasis on at-risk children. Millions of dollars are available to early childhood centers for development and improvement. According to Secretary of Education Margaret Spellings, "A child who can read is a child who can learn. And a child who can learn is a child who can succeed in school and in life" (U.S. Department of Education, 2006, p. 1). The ERF goals regarding early childhood environments of excellence are to provide preschool-age children with cognitive learning opportunities in high-quality language and literature-rich environments.

RESEARCH THAT EARLY CHILDHOOD TEACHERS CAN USE TO CREATE CENTERS OF EXCELLENCE

The following section will guide educators through an environment of excellence inventory. Following the inventory is a list of environmental suggestions for educators who want to create high-quality and literature-rich environments following the components of ERF and No Child Left Behind (NCLB) initiatives. The next section will guide you through research that will help you learn about the following:

- Enriched Early Childhood Environments Inventory
- Enriched Learning Environments Integrated With Core Components of ERF

Characteristics of high-quality programs that should be included to prepare young children for later academic success are listed in Table 6.1. Educators who also want to evaluate their program based on professional, curriculum, physical, and psychological characteristics can use Table 6.1 as a checklist.

Table 6.1 Enriching Early Childhood Environments Inventory

Professional Characteristics of High-Quality Programs	Curriculum Characteristics of High-Quality Programs	Physical Characteristics of High-Quality Programs	Psychological Characteristics of High-Quality Programs
__ Reflect cultural and community needs	__ Teachers plan a balanced schedule with opportunity for rest and play	__ Safe, nurturing, and stimulating environments	__ Centers pay attention to health care needs of the children
__ Instruction is guided by curriculum that has a systematic focus on developing cognitive, language, and early reading and writing skills	__ Parents included in planning early educational programs	__ Children have nutritious meals and snacks	__ Supervision and guidance of loving adults
__ Teachers work from lessons and activity plans that outline the purpose	__ Interesting and challenging activities	__ Print-rich environment with a variety of good books	__ Mission and goals clearly communicated to personnel and parents
__ Instruction is intentional	__ Program has a clear statement of goals and philosophy addressing all areas of child development, including cognition and reading	__ Alphabet clearly displayed	__ Environment is highly motivational through the use of positive reinforcement
__ Balance between individual, small group, and large group activities	__ Children are engaged in purposeful and meaningful activities	__ Play and learning centers with lots of writing materials	
		__ Toys conducive to imaginative play	

The Enriching Early Childhood Environments Inventory can provide useful information based on the criteria established by ERF. Educators can use the inventory as follows:

- To evaluate existing programs
- As a guideline for creating new early childhood centers
- To communicate clear objectives to parents in the area of professional, curricular, physical, and psychological characteristics of the center
- To evaluate existing programs for print-rich environments that support early literacy development based on ERF (See Table 6.2 for a list of materials to include in a print-rich environment.)
- To evaluate programs for areas of improvement to obtain funding through the ERF grants, which are available through the U.S. Department of Education

Table 6.2   Print-Rich Environments

Type of Print Materials	*Benefits for Preschool Children*
Atlas	Learn about the world and what maps look like
Comic books	Enjoy creative language and understand what characters are thinking. Learn about the concept of dialogue
Children's picture dictionary	English language learners begin to make word associations
Encyclopedia	I recommend very old ones so children can cut the pictures up
Grocery lists, receipts, and words from food items	Learn how literacy is integrated in our life
Joke books	To encourage humor
Children's magazines	To use to promote areas of interest with children such as science
Newspapers	How language is used to communicate information
Quotation books	To be inspired by others
Recipe books	To learn how math and literacy work together
Travel brochures	To learn about the world
Things doctors use; x-rays	Understand how scientific information and medical data are used by professionals
Big books	For active participation with students
Historical documents	Learn how information was communicated in the past
Lots of class-made books	To build community
Old post cards and letters	Understand how writing is used to keep in touch with others
CD-ROM books	To have interactive opportunities with literature and technology
Lego and game-building instructions	To learn how to read informational print and put things together
Menus	Understand how to read a menu
Interactive board books	To provide multisensory experiences
Books made out of unusual materials like fabric or leather	Provide interest and motivation for reading
Safety tips	Recognize harmful materials
Journals	To integrate reading and writing
Calendars	Recognize days of the week

Photograph 6.1 is an excellent example of using nonfiction materials and magazines.

Photo 6.1   Enriched Learning Environments Integrated With Core Components of Early Reading First

Using the Enriching Early Childhood Environments Inventory as a starting point to evaluate early childhood environments will help focus on program goals that integrate the core components of ERF. Following are specific examples of how the major components can be woven into the fabric of the classroom. The lessons to increase oral language give ideas on how to design literacy centers in the classroom. Although the lessons are geared for preschool-age programs, they are designed to develop oral language. Therefore, the lessons might seem challenging or inappropriate; however, it is the teacher who understands how to make appropriate modifications.

Expressive and Receptive Oral Language Development

Early childhood centers of excellence promote expressive and receptive oral language development by demonstrating they value oral language.

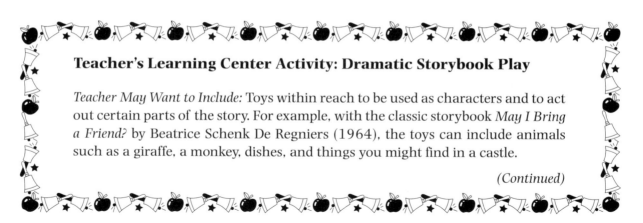

Teacher's Learning Center Activity: Dramatic Storybook Play

Teacher May Want to Include: Toys within reach to be used as characters and to act out certain parts of the story. For example, with the classic storybook *May I Bring a Friend?* by Beatrice Schenk De Regniers (1964), the toys can include animals such as a giraffe, a monkey, dishes, and things you might find in a castle.

(Continued)

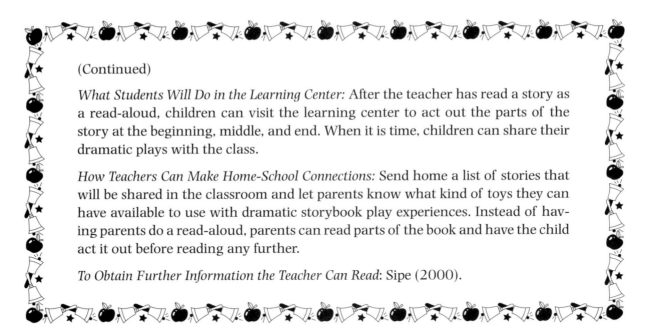

(Continued)

What Students Will Do in the Learning Center: After the teacher has read a story as a read-aloud, children can visit the learning center to act out the parts of the story at the beginning, middle, and end. When it is time, children can share their dramatic plays with the class.

How Teachers Can Make Home-School Connections: Send home a list of stories that will be shared in the classroom and let parents know what kind of toys they can have available to use with dramatic storybook play experiences. Instead of having parents do a read-aloud, parents can read parts of the book and have the child act it out before reading any further.

To Obtain Further Information the Teacher Can Read: Sipe (2000).

Once students feel comfortable acting in smaller groups, they will build confidence and feel more comfortable engaging in discussions during read-aloud experiences. The next integrated learning center integrates parent volunteers and is especially useful because it integrates high-quality literature with parental support while focusing on oral language development.

Teacher's Learning Center Activity: Moment-in-Moment Read-Alouds

Teacher May Want to Include: Parent volunteers can be used to read storybooks in small group settings at this discussion-learning center. Teachers should have available in the learning center lots of theme-based books using a variety of genres such as fiction and nonfiction. A fiction book that children like reading is *Read Anything Good Lately?* by Susan Allen and Jane Lindaman (2003). This book talks about what things children like to read, so the learning center can include rich literature such as maps, journals, newspapers, and an atlas.

What Students Will Do in the Learning Center: Students will listen to the parent volunteer but participate as much as two-thirds of the time, with one-third of the time spent in discussion after the book is read. Instruct parents to not just sit and have the children listen to the book intently but to invite conversation throughout the story. If a child is reminded of a personal experience during the story, it is okay to take a tangent and listen and discuss stories, returning to the book when appropriate.

How Teachers Can Make Home-School Connections: Teachers can share the reading experience with parents and invite them to use the same procedures at home. Extended activities related to *Read Anything Good Lately?* can be found at Millbrook Press. Parents will find scavenger hunt activities that can be used at the library and other helpful resources.

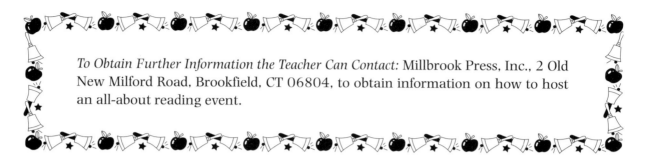

To Obtain Further Information the Teacher Can Contact: Millbrook Press, Inc., 2 Old New Milford Road, Brookfield, CT 06804, to obtain information on how to host an all-about reading event.

Oral language is the first natural literacy process children develop. Children, prior to kindergarten, delight in pretend play. Creative expression of language is important to young children. Creative expression of language also helps them develop metacognitive thinking, because they are learning how to think from the author's perspective (Block & Israel, 2004). The next learning center focuses on helping children develop oral language by using creative expression to think metacognitively.

Teacher's Learning Center Activity: Expressive Dialogic Reading

Teacher May Want to Include: In this center, children are learning how to have a conversation with other peers. After reading a story that is written in the form of another perspective or voice like the story *Detective LaRue* by Mark Teague (2004), the teacher can have the children discuss places Detective LaRue can escape in the book or create their own mystery and pretend to be Detective LaRue. The center should be an informal environment with chairs or pillows for discussion. Dog puppets may also be included in the center so children can pretend to be the voice of the characters in the book. When using this book, the learning center can be filled with nonfiction books and travel brochures from various locations in their community or state.

What Students Will Do in the Learning Center: Using creative oral language expressions, children can learn to have conversations with peers in an informal setting.

How Teachers Can Make Home-School Connections: Detective LaRue is written in a letter style writing. Teachers can send home a letter, similar to the ones in the book, and ask parents questions about how they might solve the mystery. Parent responses can be read after children have an opportunity to discuss the different escapes described in the story.

To Obtain Further Information the Teacher Can Read: Doyle & Bramwell (2006) to learn more about interactive oral reading environments. Teachers can also read another book by the same author called *Dear Mrs. LaRue* (2002).

Oral language development can easily be incorporated into daily activities. The high-quality literacy centers suggested above meet the program goals of ERF in that they utilize high-quality literature, instruction is intentionally designed to develop oral language skills, and the activities are interactive and conducive to imaginative play.

Alphabetic Knowledge

ERF initiatives emphasize that in childhood programs of excellence, teaching alphabetic principles are integrated with daily literacy activities. Recall that students acquire alphabetic knowledge when letter-sound relationships are made. When students learn about the relationship of letters and sounds and learn how to apply this knowledge to reading, this is technically referred to as phonics. Phonics provides the knowledge of all subsequent reading.

The literacy centers in this section support the integration of the alphabetic principle. All of the literacy centers below include ideas on how to use a preschool word wall to increase alphabetic knowledge. The letters of the alphabet should be placed above the word wall for quick reference and visual representation to pictures and letters. Tips on using word walls in early childhood centers include the following:

- Make sure alphabet letters above words are large and at eye level
- When possible, use alphabet letters that children can touch
- Begin the word wall with only names of children
- Place words children know on the word wall
- Use pictures with words
- Place favorite food names on the word wall
- Put names of book characters, pets, teachers, and other important people on the word wall (Brabham & Villaume, 2001)

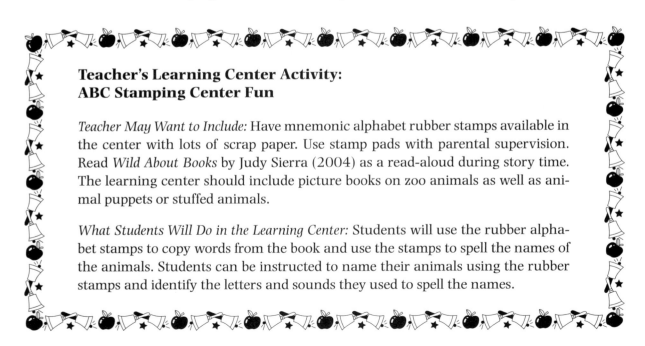

Teacher's Learning Center Activity:
ABC Stamping Center Fun

Teacher May Want to Include: Have mnemonic alphabet rubber stamps available in the center with lots of scrap paper. Use stamp pads with parental supervision. Read *Wild About Books* by Judy Sierra (2004) as a read-aloud during story time. The learning center should include picture books on zoo animals as well as animal puppets or stuffed animals.

What Students Will Do in the Learning Center: Students will use the rubber alphabet stamps to copy words from the book and use the stamps to spell the names of the animals. Students can be instructed to name their animals using the rubber stamps and identify the letters and sounds they used to spell the names.

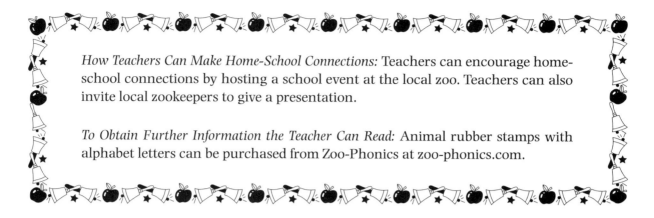

How Teachers Can Make Home-School Connections: Teachers can encourage home-school connections by hosting a school event at the local zoo. Teachers can also invite local zookeepers to give a presentation.

To Obtain Further Information the Teacher Can Read: Animal rubber stamps with alphabet letters can be purchased from Zoo-Phonics at zoo-phonics.com.

The next learning center focuses on developing the alphabetic principle using jumbo ABC reading rods. This center meets the goals of ERF because it emphasizes creative expression with letters and sounds. The center also focuses on developing sociocultural concepts.

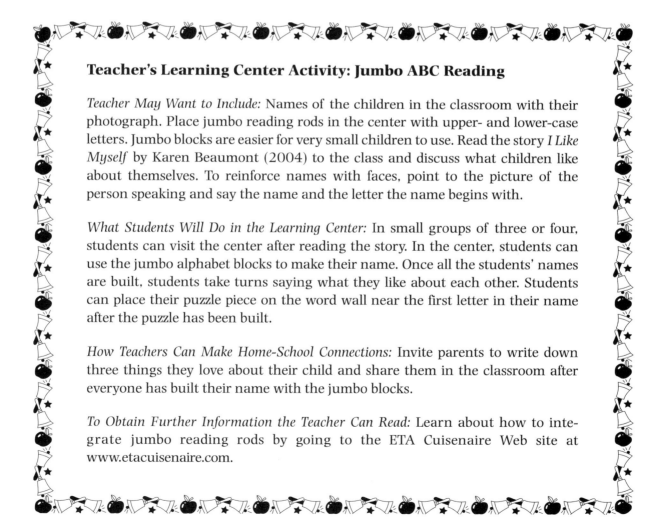

Teacher's Learning Center Activity: Jumbo ABC Reading

Teacher May Want to Include: Names of the children in the classroom with their photograph. Place jumbo reading rods in the center with upper- and lower-case letters. Jumbo blocks are easier for very small children to use. Read the story *I Like Myself* by Karen Beaumont (2004) to the class and discuss what children like about themselves. To reinforce names with faces, point to the picture of the person speaking and say the name and the letter the name begins with.

What Students Will Do in the Learning Center: In small groups of three or four, students can visit the center after reading the story. In the center, students can use the jumbo alphabet blocks to make their name. Once all the students' names are built, students take turns saying what they like about each other. Students can place their puzzle piece on the word wall near the first letter in their name after the puzzle has been built.

How Teachers Can Make Home-School Connections: Invite parents to write down three things they love about their child and share them in the classroom after everyone has built their name with the jumbo blocks.

To Obtain Further Information the Teacher Can Read: Learn about how to integrate jumbo reading rods by going to the ETA Cuisenaire Web site at www.etacuisenaire.com.

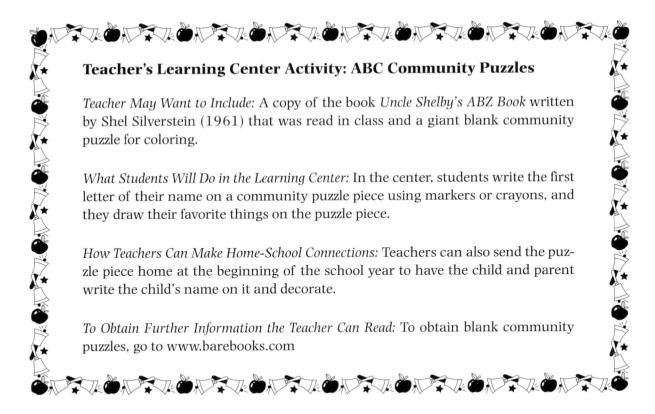

Teacher's Learning Center Activity: ABC Community Puzzles

Teacher May Want to Include: A copy of the book *Uncle Shelby's ABZ Book* written by Shel Silverstein (1961) that was read in class and a giant blank community puzzle for coloring.

What Students Will Do in the Learning Center: In the center, students write the first letter of their name on a community puzzle piece using markers or crayons, and they draw their favorite things on the puzzle piece.

How Teachers Can Make Home-School Connections: Teachers can also send the puzzle piece home at the beginning of the school year to have the child and parent write the child's name on it and decorate.

To Obtain Further Information the Teacher Can Read: To obtain blank community puzzles, go to www.barebooks.com

Integrating the alphabetic principle in everyday literacy activities reinforces what students are learning about letter-sound relationships. The learning centers in this section have focused on centers of excellence that pay attention to emotional needs of the children by building self-esteem, develop expressive creativity, and are integrated in a print-rich environment.

Phonological Awareness

Professional development is a key factor in developing centers for excellence, according to the U.S. Department of Education. Early childhood educators who want to include parents in the classroom for support and to build home-school connections can provide helpful hints on how to develop phonological awareness when working with children in learning centers. The purpose of this section is to help create an environment that stimulates development in phonological awareness by providing knowledge to parents who are working with young children. Below are six helpful research-based tips that educators can give to parents who are working at learning centers.

Teaching Tip #1: Phonological awareness is the awareness of sounds of words and the ability to detect and manipulate units (Harris & Hodges, 1995). When working with children, attention to skills that develop phonological awareness should be integrated within the context of authentic learning experiences, which means during a read-aloud experience or when a child might be telling a story (Cassady & Smith, 2004).

Teaching Tip #2: Phonemic awareness is the ability to think about intentionally individual phonemes or sounds within words and syllables. Phonemic awareness is acquired over time by activities that focus on rhyming, segmentation, and categorization through songs, games, and other activities that highlight word-learning skills (Scarborough & Brady, 2002).

Teaching Tip #3: When helping children develop phonemic awareness, it is important to understand that generally short vowels are taught before long vowels. Consonants can be taught in the context of familiar names and words. The letters of the alphabet are not to be taught in alphabetical order. According to Fry (2004), the top 10 high-frequency vowels (in order) are short *i*, short *a*, short *e*, schwa with *r*, long *o*, long *e*, short *u*, short *o*, long *a*, and long *u*. Consonants with the highest frequency are *r, t, n, s, 1, c, d, p, m,* and *b*.

Teaching Tip #4: Children who might be at risk for reading development at an early age require a different approach to learning about sounds and letters, which eventually leads to the spelling of words. It is recommended that early at-risk children receive phonemic awareness that only focuses on repeated use of one or two skills such as segmenting words into phonemes and blending phonemes to form words. At an early age, it is more important to master only a few skills (Ehri, Nunes, Willows, Schuster, Yaghoub-Zadeh et al., 2001).

Teaching Tip #5: When working with early preschool children who are developing phonemic awareness, educators and parents should pay attention to which skills are taught. The skills that are easier for children should be taught first, with the harder skills taught with more advanced learners (Ehri et al., 2001). Following is a list of skills from easiest to hardest. Teachers and parents should take into account task difficulty when working on phonemic awareness skills.

1. First sound comparison: identifying the names of pictures beginning with the same sound.

2. Blending onset-rime units into real words

3. Blending phonemes into real words

4. Deleting phoneme and saying the word that remains

5. Segmenting words into phonemes

6. Blending phonemes into nonwords.

Teaching Tip #6: The best environmental conditions for teaching phonemic awareness occur when instructional time lasts between 5 to 18 hours total and only when teaching one or two skills at a time. This should always be done in small group situations like the learning center model (Ehri et al., 2001).

Below is a sample learning center that integrates the teaching tips with phonological awareness with high-quality literature.

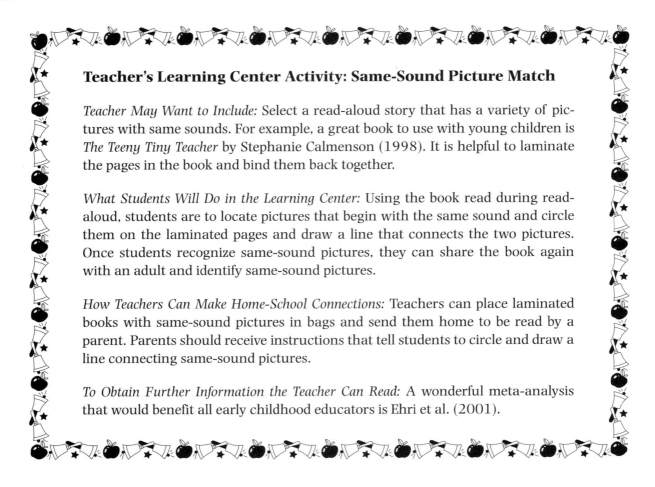

Teacher's Learning Center Activity: Same-Sound Picture Match

Teacher May Want to Include: Select a read-aloud story that has a variety of pictures with same sounds. For example, a great book to use with young children is *The Teeny Tiny Teacher* by Stephanie Calmenson (1998). It is helpful to laminate the pages in the book and bind them back together.

What Students Will Do in the Learning Center: Using the book read during read-aloud, students are to locate pictures that begin with the same sound and circle them on the laminated pages and draw a line that connects the two pictures. Once students recognize same-sound pictures, they can share the book again with an adult and identify same-sound pictures.

How Teachers Can Make Home-School Connections: Teachers can place laminated books with same-sound pictures in bags and send them home to be read by a parent. Parents should receive instructions that tell students to circle and draw a line connecting same-sound pictures.

To Obtain Further Information the Teacher Can Read: A wonderful meta-analysis that would benefit all early childhood educators is Ehri et al. (2001).

Provide parents who will be helping in centers with a copy of the parent teaching tips. You can also photocopy the tips and laminate them. The cards can be placed on a key ring and stored in a parent volunteer basket.

Print Awareness

Print awareness can easily be developed in the context of the daily literacy activities. Below is a list of six strategies that early childhood educators can integrate in the learning center environment.

1. In print-rich learning centers with lots of books that are of interest to students, print awareness skills can be developed by working with letters and words within books.

2. Students can learn about the structure and directionality by making their own books (Strickland & Schickedanz, 2004).

3. With English language learners, use predictable books such as Eric Carle's *Have You Seen My Cat* (1988) and allow them to use native language when participating (Garcia, 2000).

4. Watch *Between the Lions* (2000) available through the Public Broadcasting System. Books are read with thematic topics. One of the

characters is Click the Mouse, who takes characters from the stories on the show to out-of-book experiences. Kids can learn about the concepts of books through the integration of media and literacy.

5. Teach parents how to read storybooks with their child and point out print awareness skills while reading (Pressley, 2002).

6. Learning centers should include a variety of print-rich material, writing tables, and functional signs that have meaning for children that help to communicate the important message of books and how to read them (Neuman, 2004).

Teacher's Learning Center Activity: Picture Book Print Awareness

Teacher May Want to Include: The book called *I Love My Little Storybook* by Anita Jeram (2002) has a set of print awareness functional signs such as the one shown in Figure 6.1 and an oral explanation of what the print awareness functional signs mean and the reason for using them.

The teacher can make other signs by combining digital photographs and captions such as the following:

This book is meaningful to me because . . .

When I read, I turn the pages from . . .

When I see white space, this means . . .

I can identify page numbers.

I can identify when sentences start and end.

I understand what a word is.

I know what type of book I am reading.

I know the direction of up from down when reading a book.

I understand the structure of this book because . . .

What Students Will Do in the Learning Center: Use the print awareness signs when looking at books in the learning center and perform the task in order when looking at the books. Students can also place the cards in the books to use as bookmarks to identify that they understand the meaning of the print awareness functional sign.

(Continued)

(Continued)

How Teachers Can Make Home-School Connections: The print awareness functional cards can be sent home with parents to reinforce the skills in the classroom related to print awareness.

To Obtain Further Information, the Teacher Can Read: D. Strickland and J. A. Schickedanz (2004) to learn more about print awareness activities appropriate for early childhood students.

Figure 6.1   Example of Print Awareness Functional Sign

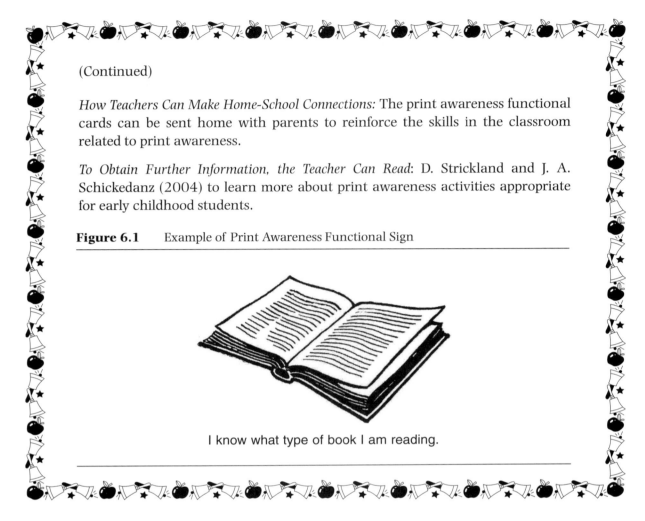

I know what type of book I am reading.

Developing Emerging Metacognitive and Scientific Minds

Helping students develop metacognitive awareness at an early age will increase children's understanding of phonemic awareness (Israel, Block, Bauserman, & Kinnucan-Welsch, 2005). When reading storybooks with children, it is important to keep in mind questions that will elicit metacognitive thinking (Israel, Bauserman, & Block, 2005). Below is a list of metacognitive prompts you can use when reading fiction and nonfiction books.

When Reading Fiction Books, Increase Metacognitive Thinking by Saying

- Before I start reading this book, I am going to think about a similar experience when I . . .
- I remember when . . .
- While we were reading, this made me think about . . .
- When we were reading this story, it made me feel . . .
- I was confused when the character . . .
- This story is important when we discuss . . .

When Reading Nonfiction Books,
Increase Metacognitive Thinking by Saying

- This topic is important to us because . . .
- When I see the word . . . I think about . . .
- The purpose for reading this book is . . .
- What do you know about this topic?
- This book is interesting because . . .

HOW TO GET STARTED WITH DESIGNING EARLY LITERACY ENVIRONMENTS OF EXCELLENCE

This section combines the information in the previous chapters with strategies that will guide you on how to design and develop your own early literacy center of excellence.

On an annual basis, since the inception of ERF, the U.S. Department of Education provides to the public a synopsis of ERF Grantees. Following is a summary of the 2005 synopsis of what other early childhood centers from around the country have established as their goals and professional development. Two key aspects required by ERF for centers and programs trying to achieve excellence are (1) to establish Project Goals for the early childhood environment and (2) engage educators in professional development.

My rationale for providing you with this information is to help you understand some of the goals and professional development plans that are being implemented around the country. It is my hope that in communicating to you, you will be more informed when making decisions. The summary can be used as a checklist to identify existing strengths or areas for improvement.

Summary of Frequently Occurring Goals from 2005 Grant Recipients

- Enhance environments with content-rich, theme-based curriculum
- Give instruction that emphasizes oral language production and emergent literacy
- Give sustained training, coaching, mentoring to build each participating teacher's capacity
- Introduce and use assessment-monitoring tools
- Accelerate development of children's language, cognitive, and literacy skills
- Build a site-based professional development system
- Nourish a highly collaborative culture that supports learning from data and research
- Help children who are experiencing difficulty in transition to kindergarten
- Provide parents with literacy training in a meaningful way
- Execute a strong management system that will include feedback and continuous improvement strategies

- Provide low-income families with a comprehensive research-based early literacy curriculum that includes oral language, cognitive development, and early reading skill development
- Integrate informational literacy in the content areas
- Improve the identified preschoolers' performances in the use of oral language, phonological awareness, print awareness, and alphabet knowledge

Summary of Frequently Occurring Professional Development Plans

- ERF mentors/coaches will support instructional strategies and assessments.
- The _____ program will build on the alignment in curriculum, strategies, professional development, and assessment.
- Training will focus on ensuring full implementation of the project curriculum, effective teaching strategies, print and language-rich classroom environments, and effective monitoring of children.
- Professional development will include intensive coaching of all classroom staff one day per week.
- At least 45 hours of formal instruction and 75 hours of individual instruction will be given.
- Professional development to support the entire program will reflect the needs of the target audience.
- Teachers will engage in over 200 hours of professional development experiences yearly.
- Professional development activities will include six credit hours from the university.

RESOURCES TO GET YOU STARTED

Establishing Goals and Mission

Use the following worksheets to begin planning for early childhood centers, professional development, or programs of excellence. Table 6.3 can be used to outline your goals and the actions you will take to achieve those goals. Once you have decided your goals, begin thinking about a mission statement. Use Table 6.4 to focus on crafting a mission that reflects the goals of your program.

Preparing for Professional Development Sessions

Once you have established your goals and mission statement, professional development will need to be considered. The following is a sample of what a lesson on phonemic awareness might look like. Parents can also be included in the professional development session.

Table 6.3   Centers of Excellence Literacy Planning Sheet

	Action
Goals	Professional Goals
	Curriculum Goals
	Physical Goals
	Psychological Goals
Literacy Assessments	Oral Language: Alphabetic Principle: Phonological Awareness: Print Awareness:
Professional Resources Needed	
Strategies for Home-School Connections	

Table 6.4   Sample Mission Outline

Use the following outline to guide your thinking about your mission statement.

I. Discover
- Questions
- Punctuality
- Courtesy

II. Guide
- Assignments
- Academic Honesty
- Professionalism

III. Serve
- Accept Diversity
- Look for Service Opportunities
- Integrate Spirituality

IV. Be Reflective
- Generate Creative Ideas
- Seek Wisdom Through Knowledge

It is the ability of learners to think on their own and to evaluate and create that is the sign of educational success. It is the ability of a child to engage in the search for truth that is the sign of educational progress. The value of intellectual achievement is to be measured in its own right, not against another's achievements.

—Patricia McCarthy (1996, p. 120)

Sample Lesson Plan for Professional Development on Phonemic Awareness

Connections	Lesson connects the prior knowledge of understanding the foundations of phonemic awareness, specifically letter and sound associations.
Objectives	Build on the foundational elements of phonics concepts and be introduced to current research-based word study applications in authentic classroom situations for emerging students. Evaluate research-based cultural conditions that influence word studies for English language learners and English second-language learners.
Time Frame	Class Time Frame: 4:30–7:05 Class will be divided into three parts. Part I: Overview & Constructing Knowledge Part II: Application of Research-Based Strategies Part III: Making Connections/Reflections
Assessment	Three layers of assessment will be used. Part I: Understanding of prior knowledge related to word study applications based on discussion. Part II: Anticipation guide and use of introductory questions to assess understanding of phonics and word studies at the emergent and emerging levels (Foster, 2004). Postdiscussions to evaluate prior knowledge to construct new meaning. Part III: Assessment done at the end of class will include a one-minute free write that will respond to introductory assessments. (Ahmedova, 2004; Foster, 2004)
Tasks	**Part I: Overview/Constructing Knowledge** 4:30–4:35 Welcome, "Personal Teacher Favorites" 4:35–4:40 Overview of class objectives, introduction, quizzes returned. Snack thanks, handouts 4:40–4:50 Sharing and application of literature 4:50–5:00 Issues with phonemic awareness relative to teaching emergent literacy 5:00–5:20 Research-based phonics and word study applications at the emergent and emerging levels, theoretical framework based on IRA Position Statement that students have read the week prior and discussed in a Balanced Literacy Framework. **Part II: Application** 5:20–5:50 Group 1 Word Study Activities/Child Study Inquiry Groups 5:50–6:20 Group 2 Word Study Activities/Child Study Inquiry Groups 6:25–6:50 Video Choice Begins **Part III: Making Connections/Reflections** 6:50–7:05 Discussion on word study applications/issues related to emergent and emerging literacy based on class objectives. Making connections with lesson objectives. Student feedback. Students respond to initial critical thinking questions. Respond to individual questions.

Resources Needed	PowerPoint setup
	Handouts
	Post-it Notes
	Word Study Activity Packets, "What to say besides sound it out." –Primary Students
Motivational Strategies	Group Discussion
	Peer Discussions
	Learner-Centered Videos
	Small-Group Activities
	Question Board
	Engaging Environment
	Choice of Activities/Learning Centers
	Student Involvement Using Teacher Favorites
	Class Book
Adaptations to Lessons Based on Student Needs	Handouts distributed in my class to help those students who struggle with note taking. One adult learner requires more input related to helping her understand concepts. I will discreetly be monitoring her and review concepts as needed.
	Time for students who need to work at a slower pace to be given during the reflection time at the end of class. Choice of video will be given because several of the graduate students teach preschool students and others work with special needs young adolescents. Individualized instruction will be given during small-group instruction and at the end of class based on student needs. A variety of resources will be shared and selected based on class dynamics, for example, choice of literature being shared by the students.
Anticipation & Modifications	I anticipate the discussion during Part I to be longer than I have planned. If this happens, I will be adjusting my time spent discussing several of the slides. I will also be making adjustments when I ask students to respond during strategic times in the lesson. Based on the time allocated for Part II, I might anticipate one group being done early. I will permit them to begin working in their inquiry groups. I also anticipate some students being bored during the activity time, because some activities may not be appropriate for them. I have placed laptops in the room and will give students a choice of investigating online word study activities or working with me in smaller groups. I anticipate students wanting to ask me many different questions related to specific assignments. Some students have been absent and have missed instruction. I have also placed in the room a Questions Board. I will address any questions at the end of class. I also anticipate the video machine to be difficult for graduates to operate. I have trained a parent to help with the videos.
Connections	**At a Glance**
	2/9 Child Study Inquiry Presentations Groups 1, 2, 3
	2/16 Child Study Inquiry Presentations Groups 4, 5, 6
	2/23 Study Groups Meet to Review for Posttest using SPP
	Notes: Collect resources from class for Phonics Binder

Sample Lesson Plan Worksheet

Prior Connections	
Objectives	
Time Frame	
Assessment	
Tasks	
Resources Needed	
Motivational Strategies	
Adaptations to Lessons Based on Student Needs	
Anticipation & Modifications	
Connections	

PARENT TIPS ON DEVELOPING PHONEMIC AWARENESS AT HOME

(Sources used are personal experiences, research on phonemic awareness mentioned in Chapter 4, and Yopp and Yopp [2000].)

- Ask, "How many sounds do you hear?"
- Parent says, "Say all the sounds you hear."
- Use songs, chants, and word games
- Read Dr. Seuss rhymes
- Tell stories to facilitate phonemic awareness, use expression, and enunciate sounds
- Play language activities such as word sorts
- Include concrete clues like chips, beans, or tiles to identify number of sounds
- Play, "Let's think of something that rhymes with . . ."
- Clap word syllables like "mail" (clap) "box" (clap)
- Read lots of poetry books
- Spend no more than 10 to 30 minutes per activity
- Expose children to rich vocabulary
- Read lots of nursery rhymes
- Memorize nursery rhymes
- Play bingo word games
- Sort items in the kitchen by initial sounds
- Sort toys by initial sounds
- Make up silly names for stuffed animals that rhyme
- Put mystery objects of like sounds in a sack and have child sort by sounds one at a time
- Practice writing familiar letters first
- Praise by saying, "Look at the way you are . . ."
- Cut pictures out of magazines and sort by sounds
- Use comic strip titles to sort by sound
- Eat lots of Campbell's Alphabet Soup
- Use good luck charms to make words

TIPS ON SMALL GROUP DIALOGUE IN EARLY CHILDHOOD CLASSROOMS

This list of tips from recommendations by Mcintyre, Kyle, and Moore (2006) will help you think about how you approach small group dialogues.

- Be aware that talk is related to classroom culture
- Proximity should be natural, with students sitting where they can see everyone's faces
- Children should feel comfortable where their contributions are valued
- Invite children to visualize conversations they will have with the group and what they hear people talking about

- Model thinking aloud by responding to questions that you might be thinking out loud so students can hear your thinking processes
- Allow children to respond to one another without intervention
- Teach children acceptable behaviors when working in small groups
- Use laughter when appropriate and allow children to laugh
- Permit stories that make personal connections
- Use encouraging words
- Lead students when appropriate
- Encourage manners
- Do not overpraise students
- Promote collaborative work and the sharing of ideas

TEACHING TIPS FOR PARENTS AS HELPING HANDS

Teachers can provide opportunities for allowing parents to share in the planning of the center's environmental features in the following ways:

- Invite parents to share services that might enhance the center by offering to build constructions that will create inviting literacy centers. For example, if you have a parent who is in construction, elicit that parent's support in building a ministage or theater where children can present plays they write and create.
- Teachers can make home-school connections by sending home weekly newsletters and praising children for accomplishments made during the week. This will help parents reinforce the praise the child is receiving at school at home.
- Invite parents to donate supplies to a writing center. The list might include scrap paper, envelopes, interesting writing tools, magazines, quotes, favorite books, blank books to write in, old journals, craft supplies to make books, and anything else that might enhance a writing center.
- Working parents might have difficulty feeling part of the center's environment. Teachers can keep this in mind and present home volunteer opportunities that can be sent back to school such as making bulletin boards at home, creating interesting displays, cutting items for seasonal art projects that will be hung during parent events, and growing plants at home for children to take care of in school.

LITERACY TREASURE CHEST

Poetry has always been a favorite type of genre with children, as many of the first books they heard would have been nursery rhyme books. This chapter concludes with a collection of literacy center ideas that can be used with poetry books.

Poetry Starters: Fill a box of phrases that students have cut out of magazines, famous quotes from poets, or adjectives that students have written down on index cards. Have students use the resources for brainstorming ideas for a poem.

Funny Title Time: On an index card, have students write down silly titles or cut titles out of the newspaper that sound funny. Use the title starters to help students get started on their poetry.

Poetry Picture Ideas: Have a parent volunteer fill cereal boxes full of theme-related pictures. You can laminate the pictures to keep them longer. Students can use the pictures as a springboard for describing characters or setting in a poem. The visual aid will help students be more descriptive in their writing.

Poets on Stage: Have students read and act out poems that they have written or simply enjoy reading. Encourage the use of oral language and expression when reading poems. If the noise disrupts the other students, teach students how to use their whisper voices while on stage.

SUMMARY

In this book, you have learned about the key components of ERF and how to integrate the components in literacy that occur throughout the school day and at home. You have achieved the goals of this book by accomplishing the following:

- Learning about key strategies on how to increase oral language development at an early age and how to use print-rich material to develop oral language confidence

- Learning the principles of alphabetic knowledge and how to apply alphabetic knowledge in daily literacy instruction. To help reinforce the alphabetic principle, make sure there are plenty of ABC books available for children to read and look at. Table 6.5 is a list of fun multisensory ABC books that children will love.

- Learning how to teach children the functions of a book and the directionality of how books are read

- Learning about key strategies that can increase metacognitive awareness in literacy applications with young children

Now it is your turn to take what you have learned from this book and apply it in the classroom with young children. One way to get started is by creating your daily schedule. You can use the template in Table 6.6 to get started. The two-dimensional planning schedule helps you think about what happens in the physical environment and corresponding instructional goals that guide centers of excellence one day at a time!

Table 6.5 Multisensory ABC Books to Reinforce the Alphabetic Principle

The Hidden Alphabet by Laura Vaccaro Seeger (2003). Brookfield, CT: A Neal Porter Book.	This book has cut-out shapes with hidden alphabet pictures that children can find before they open the book flap to see what letter it is. Done in black with a border with bright pictures.
ABC Look at Me by Roberta Grobel Intrater (2005). New York: Price Stern Sloan.	This interactive board book has alphabet letters associated with feelings. Under cut-out squares are real photos of children demonstrating the feeling with facial expressions.
F is for Fiesta by Susan Middleton Elya (2006). New York: G. P. Putnam's Sons.	What an excellent book to use to teach about multiculturalism and words in Spanish and English.
The Upside-Down Alphabet Book by Lisa Campbell Ernst (2004) New York: Simon & Schuster.	The text is written around the letters of the alphabet so that children can interact with the book and think differently by making associations to other objects.
Alpha Bugs by David A. Carter (1994). New York: Simon & Schuster.	Another great interactive board book with alphabet letters that pop up. The pictures represent mnemonics for the alphabet letters. A truly fabulous must-have book for preschool children.
ABC Pop! by Rachel Isadora (1999). New York: Viking.	Alphabet letters are with everyday things that children could discover in their world. The letters are placed with sounds so the children can make letter-sound associations to help develop phonemic awareness.
Pilobolus: The Human Alphabet Photographs by John Kane (2005). New Milford, CT: Roaring Brooks Press.	A great book for children who learn best through kinesthetic senses. The letters of the alphabet are all made with people. While reading this book, children can participate by trying to make the letters. An excellent interactive book!

Table 6.6 Two-Dimensional Early Childhood Daily Literacy Planning Guide

Physical Setting	*Instructional Goals*
Environmental Literacy	Literacy Task Goals
Materials	Early Reading First Skills:
Procedures for Morning Integrated Thematic Work	**Procedures for Afternoon Integrated Thematic Work**
Morning Silent Reading	Afternoon Meeting
Morning Meeting	Interactive Read-Aloud Selection

Physical Setting	Instructional Goals
Overview of The Day 1. 2. 3. Read-Aloud Selection	Project Sharing Special Subjects:
Small-Group Lesson Block 1. Writing Center 2. Research Center 3. Publishing Center 4. Performing Arts Center 5. Creativity Center 6. Home-School Connections Volunteer Center 7. Teacher Discovery Discussions **Transition Notes:**	**Small-Group Lesson Block** 1. Writing Center 2. Research Center 3. Publishing Center 4. Performing Arts Center 5. Creativity Center 6. Home-School Connections Volunteer Center 7. Teacher Discovery Discussions **Transition Notes:**
Lunch & Activity Break Teacher Notes	**Closing Connections** Student Compliments Student Reminders Teacher Notes

SOURCE: Inspired by personal teaching experiences, research from the U.S. Department of Education, teacher reflections, and research on picture storybooks by Sipe (2000).

Resources

A FACILITATOR'S GUIDE TO PLANNING AND ORGANIZING FOR AN ENGAGING AND MOTIVATING PROFESSIONAL DEVELOPMENT DAY

This appendix includes tips that will enable facilitators to guide small group or large group sessions with little planning. The tips will successfully guide the study of this book. The schedule can easily be adapted for whole-day professional development sessions or half-day professional development sessions. For facilitators who would like more information on practical strategies for small or large group sessions, Corwin Press publishes a free 16-page resource titled *Tips for Facilitators* that can be downloaded from their Web site at www.corwinpress.com under Other Resources.

Below is a checklist of tasks you might need to consider prior to your professional development day.

How to Motivate and Engage Teachers in the Professional Development Day

Prior to planning your professional development session, administer the Early Childhood Literacy Needs Assessment to those who will be in attendance. I developed the needs assessment when I was a facilitator for my first teacher inservice day. I wanted the teachers to feel like the inservice was meaningful to them. I administered a version of the needs assessment below a week before the scheduled professional day. To motivate teachers to return the assessment, the school principal enticed them with raffle prizes during the inservice. If teachers returned the assessment, they would be eligible for a raffle prize. We used children's picture books and a variety of gift certificates for the raffles. We also took donations from the community. Use the form below and modify it based on what type of information you would like to obtain from the teachers.

A Checklist of What to Do to Prepare
for Your Professional Development Day

_____ **Administer Early Childhood Literacy Needs Assessment** Prior to planning and facilitating a study session on this book, the Early Childhood Literacy Needs Assessment should be administered to those in attendance at the session. The purpose of the Early Childhood Literacy Needs Assessment is to obtain information about what teachers feel are strengths or areas of weaknesses that need to be addressed during the professional development session. Knowing in advance what the needs of teachers are will help you scaffold your presentation to meet their needs as well as build in opportunities to discuss topics of interest from this book. Communicate when you would like the needs assessment returned.

_____ **Plan Session Format** Decide if you are planning a small group or whole group discussion and a whole-day or half-day session format.

_____ **Prepare Conducive Professional Development Environment** Depending on the type of session format you are planning and the number of teachers attending, you will need to make arrangements in advance for a location that suits your needs. The materials in this section will require you to have an overhead available. Regardless of the session format, the tips included in this session use peer discussion as a method of instruction. Therefore, the tables should be arranged in small groups of five to six, depending on the size.

_____ **Communicate Professional Development Session to Teachers** After key decisions have been made, communicate to those who will be attending the date, time, and location. You will also need to let them know what materials they need to prepare in advance. If you are using this book as a book study, communicate your expectations in advance.

_____ **Get Organized** Prepare a folder or place to keep your presentation materials.

_____ **Schedule a Planning Session** If you are working with others to plan the professional development session, you will need to schedule a planning session to review objectives, analyze the needs assessments to make decisions about your presentation, and delegate tasks.

_____ **Consider Other Tasks** Think about other tasks you might need to complete prior to the professional development day. Do you need to order supplies? Will you have raffle prizes? Will you provide snacks or drinks? Will teachers need writing supplies? Do you need to obtain name tags? Will you have a seating chart? Do you have backup plans in case something or someone is unable to present?

_____ **Obtain Free Resources** Visit the U.S. Department of Education and request resources on ERF.

_____ Planning Notes

Sample Early Childhood Literacy Needs Assessment

1. What does an A-Plus (pseudonym) school do well in the area of literacy development?

2. What types of literacy activities do students enjoy?

3. In what areas can an A-Plus school improve in the area if literacy?

4. What are your professional development needs in literacy?

5. What are three literacy goals that you think an A-Plus school should consider this year?

EARLY CHILDHOOD LITERACY NEEDS ASSESSMENT

(Using this book as a book study selection to be read prior to the professional development day)

1. Based on the information you read in the book, what does an A-Plus school do well in the area of oral language development, alphabetic knowledge, phonemic awareness, and print awareness?

2. What types of activities in the book would you like to learn more about?

3. Based on what you have read, what areas can an A-Plus school improve?

4. What type of professional development experiences would benefit you most?

5. What are three goals that you think an A-Plus school should consider this year?

6. Comments or suggestions

How to Analyze the Needs Assessment Data

A sample needs assessment from the results of my inservice are summarized below. This summary can be useful for facilitators when trying to organize their results in a meaningful way. After I compiled the needs assessment, I organized the presentation around the needs most important in the allocated time. For some areas that needed to be addressed, like writing prompts for students, I gave them a handout and we generated our own writing prompts that same day. Prior to beginning the workshop, three index cards were passed out to the teachers. While everyone was arriving and getting settled, teachers were asked to write down three writing prompts they could use in the classroom. The school used the teacher-generated writing prompts to publish their own A-Plus School Writing Prompts book. When you are reviewing the needs assessment, determine what information is most important and needs to be addressed during the session. You will also need to determine if anything can be addressed in a handout.

Depending on how you are using this book in your presentation, you will need to rewrite the needs assessment to reflect your intentions for using this book. Following is a list of how you can use this book prior to your scheduled professional development day.

- In study groups based on grade level, teachers can read selected chapters that are pertinent to them.
- You can use the book as a resource to start the school year and assign to be read prior to the first day of school.
- You can provide a copy of the book for each teacher to read independently.
- If funds are limited, place a few copies in the office and allow teachers to check them out several weeks in advance.
- You can coordinate with another school and do a book swap, where you purchase one professional development resource and the other school purchases a different title. When you are finished, you can swap the books.
- Invite parents and teachers to do a book study and use this text as one of the selections

Sample Summary of Needs Assessment

Below is a sample of how I analyzed the data from my needs assessment results. I used the data to determine the needs that were the highest priority. Then I decided how I could efficiently address them during the professional day. Some questions to ask yourself when analyzing the needs assessment data follow:

- What questions do I need to respond to?
- What is it I want to communicate during the professional day?
- What is the purpose of the professional day?
- Why do I need to address some of the issues?
- What information do I specifically need to address immediately?
- How do I respond to personal comments that should not be shared during the presentation?
- What significant information are teachers requesting?
- How do I use the materials from this book to respond to the questions?

Summary of an A-Plus School Needs Assessment / Academic Year 2005/2006

Compiled by Susan E. Israel

Notes in parenthesis are my translations of teacher responses. (14 responses summarized)

Question	Primary (PreK–3)	Special Areas (PreK–8)
1. What does A-Plus do well in the area of literacy?	• Likes 6-traits • Incorporating 6-traits with standards	No responses or felt didn't apply
2. What literacy activities do students enjoy?	• Like journals, Friday letters, 1-1 parent mentors, writing on their own, writing lists	• Enjoy transition assignments with peers • Enjoy writing about magazine articles, like newsletters, cards, PowerPoint
3. Literacy areas A-Plus school can improve	• Need to assign more written assignments • Students need to use 6-traits on their own. *(self-regulated writing skills)* • Work on the thought processes of writing *(metacognitive writing skills)* • Daily interactive writing *(peer writing)*	• Learning how to cite references, students need to know about plagiarism • Need to see special areas integrate writing in their classes
4. Professional Development Needs	• Love hearing ideas from other teachers • More 6+1 ideas • Split into groups • Doesn't apply to Pre-K *(Pre-K will need developmentally appropriate writing ideas)*	• Writing ideas in Spanish class *(English language learners)*
5. Goals	Three teachers will share • Book ideas from workshop • Spelling stages	None
6. Comments	• First grade does not use 6+1 that often; more cost-effective approach would be better	None

NOTE Special areas include music, art, physical education, computer science, and media.

SAMPLE SCHEDULE FOR YOUR PROFESSIONAL DEVELOPMENT DAY

Based on the needs assessment of the teachers, you can use this information to scaffold your presentation. You can also assign specific chapters to be read and write your needs assessment to reflect the readings in that chapter. Following is a schedule that you can use when organizing for your day. Depending on the amount of time you have allocated for the professional development day, you can add or delete specific activities. This presentation schedule should be used as a guideline.

Sample Presentation Schedule

Title of Presentation: Learning About Early Reading First

Date/Time: 9:00 a.m.–12:00 noon

Goal: Develop an environment that supports ERF initiative and creates programs of excellence.

Prepreparation Plans: Organize the room in small groups, set up an overhead, place children's books for raffles around the room. Pass out handouts that you have selected based on your needs assessment. Set aside a table for drinks. Make your overheads.

Welcome: Use one of the quotes in this book and place it on an overhead.

Overview Presentation Goals: Explain the specific goals you hope to achieve by the end of the session. Announce the tentative schedule for the day.

Overview ERF: Using the information from the book and the topics of interest to you, scaffold your presentation about ERF initiatives. Give background information.

Share Assessment Results: It is helpful for teachers to know that what they have to say is important. Share with them the results on an overhead. Explain your rationale for the needs you are going to address during your presentation.

Invite Book Reviews: Invite participants to share what they thought was useful information in the book and why.

Address Needs: You will have flexibility here in how you approach the teachers' needs. For example, if teachers wanted to learn more about specific activities, you can demonstrate them or provide more information. I recommend you invite teachers to model several activities that they found useful.

Wrapping Up Needs: Prior to the break, bring some closure to the needs assessment and explain to them your goals for the remainder of the day. Invite teachers to share thoughts on the needs assessment. Ask if further information is needed on any of the topics. At this time, draw for raffle prizes.

Break: Length depending on time available

Key Discussion Topics on ERF: Address professional development needs. This presentation will be a segue into small group teacher discussions.

Small Group Discussions: In study groups or by tables, teachers should discuss assigned reading from the book. Depending on your goals, I suggest you allow time for discussion and time for problems/solutions or goal-setting plans for your school.

Large Group Sharing: Invite groups to share discussions or small group task.

Show Video Clip: One of my favorite videos is by Dewitt Jones (2001) called *Celebrate What's Right With the World.* I think it is important to end your presentation on a positive note as well as motivate the attendees for challenges or goal achievements that are ahead. I use the clips from the video to get them thinking about what is right about teaching rather than what is wrong.

Summary of Day: Invite teachers to share what was helpful information and what information is still needed. Your job is to provide them with the tools and confidence to create centers of excellence.

Closing Comments: Explain your thoughts on the day. Thank those who made a contribution. End with future goals that you will achieve.

Below is a planning worksheet that you can use to help you organize for your professional development day.

What to Do After the Professional Development Day

After your professional development day, you will want to wrap up any loose ends and begin planning on how you can reinforce the information gained with the teachers in the classroom and center environment. Here are a few things to consider:

- Do you need to thank anyone for help during the presentation?
- What specific information do you need to follow up on?
- Did you make any promises that you need to keep?
- What did you learn from the professional development day that will help you improve the programs for early childhood children?
- Do you need to research any specific topics?
- Will you consider obtaining feedback from the participants?

Worksheet for Professional Development Day

Title of Presentation:

Date/Time:
Goal:

Prepreparation Plans:

Welcome:

Overview Presentation Goals:

Overview Early Reading First:

Share Assessment Results:

Invite Book Reviews:

Address Needs:

Wrapping Up Needs:

Break:

Key Discussion Topics on ERF:

Small Group Discussions:

Large Group Sharing:

Show Video Clip:

Summary of Day:

Closing Comments:

References

Adams, M. J. (1995). *Beginning to read: Thinking and learning about print.* Cambridge: Massachusetts Institute of Technology Press.

Allen, S., & Lindaman, J. (2003). *Read anything good lately?* Brookfield, CT: Millbrook Press.

American Academy of Pediatrics. (2000). Children's Health Topics: Developmental Stages. Retrieved July 18, 2006, from www.medem.com

Barker, T. A., & Torgesen, J. K. (1995). An evaluation of computer-assisted instruction in phonological awareness with below average readers. *Journal of Educational Computing Research, 13*(1), 89–103.

Bauserman, K. L. (2003). Phonological awareness and print concepts: Analysis of skill acquisition by kindergarten children utilizing computer-assisted-instruction. Unpublished doctoral dissertation, Ball State University of Muncie, Indiana.

Beaumont, K. (2004). *I like myself.* San Diego, CA: Harcourt.

Bell, D., & Jarvis, D. (2002). Letting go of 'letter of the week.' *Primary Voices K-6, 11*(2), 10–24.

Bird, A., Reese, E., & Trip, G. (2006). Parent-child talk about past emotional events: Association with child temperament and goodness-of-fit. *Journal of Cognition and Development, 7,* 189–210.

Blair, C. (2002). School readiness: Integrating cognition and emotion in a neurobiological conceptualization of children's functioning at school entry. *American Psychologist, 57,* 111–127.

Block, C. C., & Israel, S. E. (2004). The ABC's of performing highly effective think-alouds. *The Reading Teacher, 58*(2), 154–167.

Block, C. C., & Israel, S. E. (2005). *Reading first and beyond: The complete guide for teachers and literacy coaches.* Thousand Oaks, CA: Corwin Press.

Block, C. C., & Israel, S. E. (2006). *Quotes to inspire great reading teachers.* Thousand Oaks, CA: Corwin Press.

Botzakis, S., & Malloy, J. A. (2006). Emergent readers. *Reading Research Quarterly, 41,* 394–403.

Brabham, E. G., & Villaume, S. K. (2001). Building walls of words. *The Reading Teacher, 54,* 7.

Brown, M. W. (1977). *The important book.* New York: Harper and Row.

Calmenson, S. (1998). *The teeny tiny teacher.* New York: Scholastic.

Cambourne, B. (2001). Conditions for literacy learning. *The Reading Teacher, 54*(8), 784–786.

Carle, E. (1988). *Have you seen my cat?* New York: Philomel Books.

Carrell, P. L., & Grabe, W. (2002). Reading. In N. Schmitt (Ed.), *An introduction to applied linguistics* (pp. 233–250). London: Edward Arnold.

Carrow-Woolfolk, E. (1995). *Oral and written language scales.* Circle Pines, MN: American Guidance Service.

Cassady, J. C., & Smith, L. L. (2004). The impact of a reading-focused integrated learning system on phonological awareness in kindergarten. *Journal of Literacy Research, 35*(4), 947–964.

Christie, J. F., Enz, B. J., & Vukelich, C. (2007). *Teaching language and literacy: Preschool through the elementary grades* (3rd ed.). Boston: Allyn & Bacon.

Clay, M. M. (1972). *Sand: The concepts about print test.* Auckland, NZ: Heinemann.

Clay, M. M. (1979). *Stones: The concepts about print test.* Auckland, NZ: Heinemann.

Clay, M. M. (1993). *An observation survey of early literacy achievement.* Portsmouth, NH: Heinemann.

Cumpiano, I. (1995). *Abuela's big bed: A Puerto Rican folktale.* Needham Heights, MA: Silver Burdett Ginn.

Cunningham, P. M. (2000). *Phonics they use* (3rd ed.). New York: Addison-Wesley.

De Regniers, B. S. (1964). *May I bring a friend?* New York: Simon & Schuster.

DeBruin-Parecki, A. (1999). *Assessing adult childhood storybook reading practices* (Tech. Rep. No. 2004). Ann Arbor: University of Michigan, Center for Improvement of Early Reading Achievement.

Donnelly, D. (2003). *Leonardo, beautiful dreamer.* New York: Dutton Children's Books.

Doyle, B. G., & Bramwell, W. (2006). Promoting emergent literacy and social-emotional learning through dialogic reading. *The Reading Teacher, 59*(6), 554–564.

Driscoll, M. (2003). *A child's introduction to poetry.* New York: Black Dog and Laventhal.

Duke, N. K. (2000). 3.6 minutes per day: The scarcity of information texts in first grade. *Reading Research Quarterly, 35*(2), 202–224.

Ediger, K., Willcutt, J., & Bohn, C. (2005). Research-based practices for oral language development. In C. C. Block & S. E. Israel (Eds.), *Reading first and beyond: The complete guide for teachers and literacy coaches* (pp. 13–28). Thousand Oaks, CA: Corwin Press.

Ehri, L. C. (1995). Phases of development in learning to read. *Journal of Research in Reading, 18,* 116–125.

Ehri, L. C., Nunes, S. R., Willows, D. M., Schuster, B. V., Yaghoub-Zadeh, Z., & Shanahan, T. (2001). Phonemic awareness instruction helps children learn to read: Evidence from the National Reading Panel's meta-analysis. *Reading Research Quarterly, 36*(3), 250–287.

Fry, E. (2004). Phonics: A large phoneme-grapheme frequency count revised. *Journal of Literacy Research, 36*(1), 85–98.

Galda, L., & Liang, L. A. (2003). Literature as experience or looking for facts: Stance in the classroom. *Reading Research Quarterly, 38*(2), 268–275.

Garcia, E. (1994). *Understanding and meeting the challenge of student diversity.* Boston: Houghton Mifflin.

García, G. E. (2000). Bilingual children's reading. In M. L. Kamil, P. B. Mosenthal, P. D. Pearson, & R. Barr (Eds.), *Handbook of reading research* (Vol. 3, pp. 813–834). Mahwah, NJ: Lawrence Erlbaum.

Harris, T. L., & Hodges, R. E. (1995). *The literacy dictionary: The vocabulary of reading and writing.* Newark, DE: International Reading Association.

Hoberman, M. (2004). *You read to me, I'll read to you.* Boston: Little, Brown.

Hresko, W. P., & Hammill, D. D. (1999). *Test of early language development* (3rd ed.). Austin, TX: Pro-Ed.

Huey, E. B. (1908). *The psychology and pedagogy of reading.* Cambridge: Massachusetts Institute of Technology Press.

Invernizzi, M., Sullivan, A., Meier, J., & Swank, L. (2004). *Phonological Awareness Literacy Screening PreK (PALS-PreK).* Charlottesville: University of Virginia. Retrieved July 18, 2006, from pals.virginia.edu

Israel, S. E., Bauserman, K., & Block, C. C. (2005). Metacognitive assessments strategies. *Thinking Classroom, 6*(2), 21–28.

Israel, S. E., Block, C. C., Bauserman, K., & Kinnucan-Welsch, K. (2005). *Metacognition in literacy learning: Theory, assessment, instruction, and professional development.* Mahwah, NJ: Lawrence Erlbaum.

Jeram, A. (2002). *My little storybook.* Vauxhall, London: Walker Books.

Johnston, P. H. (2004). *Choice words.* Portland, ME: Stenhouse.

Jones, D. (2001). *Celebrate what's right with the world* [Video]. Windsor, CA: Dewitt Jones Productions.

Justice, L. M., & Ezell, H. K. (2002). Use of storybook reading to increase print awareness in at-risk children. *American Journal of Speech-Language Pathology, 11,* 17–29.

Keats, E. J. (1962). *The snowy day.* New York: Scholastic.

Lehman, B. (2004). *The red book.* Boston: Houghton Mifflin.

Lipson, M. Y., & Wixson, K. K. (2003). *Assessment & instruction of reading and writing difficulty: An interactive approach.* Boston: Allyn & Bacon.

Liszkowski, U., Carpenter, M., Striano, T., & Tomasello, M. (2006). 12–18-month-olds point to provide information for others. *Journal of Cognition and Development, 7,* 173–187.

McCarthy, P. (1996). *The scent of jasmine: Reflections for peace in everyday life.* Collegeville, MN: The Order of Saint Benedict.

McGee, L. M., & Richgels, D. J. (2004). *Literacy's beginnings: Supporting young readers and writers* (4th ed.). Boston: Allyn & Bacon.

McIntyre, E., Kyle, D. W., & Moore, G. H. (2006). A primary-grade teacher's guidance toward small-group dialogue. *Reading Research Quarterly, 41*(1), 36–66.

Moll, L. C., & Greenberg, J. B. (1990). Creating zones of possibilities: Combining social contexts for instruction. In L. C. Moll (Ed.), *Vygotsky and education: Instructional implications and applications of sociohistorical psychology* (pp. 319–348). New York: Cambridge University Press.

Morrow, L. M., & Gambrell, L. B. (2000). Literature-based reading instruction. In M. Kamil, P. Mosenthal, P. D. Pearson, & R. Barr (Eds.), *Handbook of reading research* (Vol. 3, pp. 563–586). Mahwah, NJ: Lawrence Erlbaum.

Morrow, L. M., & Gambrell, L. B. (2004). *Using children's literature in preschool: Comprehending and enjoying books.* Newark, DE: International Reading Association.

Morrow, L. M., & Rand, M. K. (1991). Promoting literacy during play by designing early childhood classroom environments. *The Reading Teacher, 44,* 396–402.

Murray, B. A. (1998). Gaining alphabetic insight: Is phoneme manipulation skill or identity knowledge causal? *Journal of Educational Psychology, 90*(3), 461–475.

National Institute of Child Health and Human Development. (2000). Report of the National Reading Panel. Teaching children to read: An evidence-based assessment of the scientific research literature on reading and its implications for reading instruction: Reports of the subgroups (NIH Publication No. 00–4754). Washington, DC: U.S. Government Printing Office.

Neuman, S. B. (2004). The effect of print-rich classroom environments on early literacy growth. *The Reading Teacher, 58*(1), 89–91.

Neuman, S., & Roskos, K. (1990). Play, print, and purpose: Enriching play environments for literacy development. *The Reading Teacher, 44,* 214–221.

O'Connor, R. E., & Jenkins, J. R. (1995). Improving the generalization of sound/symbol knowledge: Teaching spelling to kindergarten children with disabilities. *Journal of Special Education, 29*(3), 255–275.

Pappas, C. C. (2006). The information book genre: Its role in integrated science literacy research and practice. *Reading Research Quarterly, 41*(2), 226–250.

Paris, A. H., & Paris, S. G. (2003). Assessing narrative comprehension in young children. *Reading Research Quarterly, 38*(1), 36–76.

Pressley, M. (2002). Effective beginning reading instruction. *Journal of Literacy Research, 34*(2), 165–188.

Pressley, M. (2006). *Reading instruction that works: The case for balanced teaching.* New York: Guilford Press.

Pressley, M., & Afflerbach, P. (1995). *Verbal protocols of reading: The nature of constructively responsive reading.* Hillsdale, NJ: Lawrence Erlbaum.

Prior, J., & Gerard, M. R. (2004). *Environmental print in the classroom: Meaningful connections for learning to read.* Newark, DE: International Reading Association.

Rathvon, N. (2004). *Early reading assessment: A practitioner's handbook.* New York: Guilford Press.

Reach Out and Read National Reading Center. (2000). *Reach out and read: Making books part of a healthy childhood.* Retrieved July 18, 2006, from www.reachoutandread.org

Reading Rockets. (2006). *First year teacher program: Module 1—Print awareness.* Retrieved July 26, 2006, from www.readingrockets.org/firstyear/fyt.php?CAT=30

Reitsma, P., & Wesseling, R. (1998). Effects of computer-assisted training of blending skills in kindergarteners. *Scientific Studies of Reading, 2*(4), 301–320.

Rodriguez, T. A. (2001). From the known to the unknown: Using cognates to teach English to Spanish-speaking literates. *The Reading Teacher, 54*(8), 744–746.

Rueda, R., & Yaden, D. B. (2006). The literacy education of linguistically and culturally diverse young children: An overview of outcomes, assessment, and large-scale interventions. In B. Spodek & O. N. Saracho (Eds.), *Handbook of research on the education of young children* (2nd ed., pp. 167–186). Mahwah, NJ: Lawrence Erlbaum.

Saul, W. E., & Dieckman, D. (2005). Choosing and using information trade books. *Reading Research Quarterly, 40*(4), 502–513.

Scarborough, H. S., & Brady, S. A. (2002). Toward a common terminology for talking about speech and reading: A glossary of the "phon" words and some related terms. *Journal of Literacy Research, 34*(3), 299–336.

Schickedanz, J. A., & Casbergue, R. M. (2004). *Writing in preschool: Learning to orchestrate meaning and marks.* Newark, DE: International Reading Association.

Sierra, J. (2004). *Wild about books.* New York: Alfred A. Knopf.

Silva, C., & Alves-Martins, M. (2002). Phonological skills and writing of presyllabic children. *Reading Research Quarterly, 37*(4), 466–483.

Silverstein, S. (1961). *Uncle Shelby's ABZ book.* New York: Simon & Schuster.

Sipe, L. R. (2000). The construction of literary understanding by first and second graders in oral response to picture storybook read-alouds. *Reading Research Quarterly, 35*(2), 252–275.

Soderman, A. K., Gregory, K. M., & McCarty, L. T. (2005). *Scaffolding emergent literacy: A child-centered approach for preschool through Grade 5* (2nd ed.). Boston: Allyn & Bacon.

Stahl, S. A., Duffy-Hester, A. M., & Dougherty-Stahl, K. A. (1998). Everything you wanted to know about phonics (but were afraid to ask). *Reading Research Quarterly, 33,* 338–355.

Strickland, D. (2004). The role of literacy in early childhood education. *The Reading Teacher, 58*(1), 86–100.

Strickland, D., & Schickedanz, J. A. (2004). *Learning about print in preschool: Working with letters, words, and beginning links with phonemic awareness.* Newark, DE: International Reading Association.

Sulzby, E. (1990). Assessment of emergent writing and children's language while writing. In L. M. Morrow & J. Smith (Eds.), *Assessment for instruction in early literacy.* Englewood, NJ: Prentice Hall.

Sulzby, E. (1992). Research directions: Transitions from emergent to conventional writing. *Language Arts, 69,* 290–297.

Taylor, D. (1983). *Family literacy: Young children learning to read and write.* Exeter, NH: Heinemann.

Teague, M. (2004). *Detective LaRue.* New York: Scholastic Press.

U. S. Department of Education. (2000). *Early Reading First and Reading First.* Retrieved February 13, 2006, from www.ed.gov/nclb/methods/reading/readingfirst.html

U.S. Department of Education. (2001). *Ready to read, ready to learn.* Retrieved February 14, 2006, from www.ed.gov/news/pressreleases/2001/07/07262002.html

U.S. Department of Education. (2002a). *Early Reading First.* Retrieved February 21, 2006, from ed.gov/programs/earlyreading/index.html

U.S. Department of Education. (2002b). *Healthy Start, Grow Smart Series: Information booklets from newborn through 12 months old.* Retrieved June 21, 2007, from www.ed.gov/parents/earlychild/ready/healthystart/index.html

U.S. Department of Education. (2004). *Early Reading First: Frequently asked questions.* Retrieved February 14, 2006, from www.ed.gov/programs/earlyreading/faq/html

U.S. Department of Education. (2005a). *No Child Left Behind: What parents need to know.* Retrieved June 21, 2007, from www.ed.gov/nclb/overview/intro/parents/nclb.html

U.S. Department of Education. (2005b). *Student achievement and school accountability programs* (CFDA No. 84.359B). Washington, DC: Office of Elementary and Secondary Education.

U.S. Department of Education. (2006). *Early Reading First: Frequently asked questions.* Retrieved February 14, 2006, from www.ed.gov/programs/earlyreading/faq.html

U.S. President's Advisory Commission on Educational Excellence for Hispanic Americans. (2003). *From risk to opportunity: Fulfilling the educational needs of Hispanic Americans in the 21st Century.* Retrieved June 21, 2007, from www.yic.gov/paceea/finalreport.pdf

Vukelich, C., Christie, J., & Enz, B. F. (2007). *Helping young children learn language and literacy: Birth through kindergarten.* Boston: Allyn & Bacon.

Waldbart, A., Meyers, B., & Meyers, J. (2006). Invitations to families in an early literacy support program. *The Reading Teacher, 59*(8), 774–785.

Wargin, K. (2004). *M is for melody: A music alphabet.* Chelsea, MI: Sleeping Bear Press.

WGBH Boston, Sirius Thinking, Ltd., & Mississippi Public Broadcasting. (Producers). *Between the Lions* [Television series]. Boston: WGBH.

Williams, T. K. (1997). *Expressive vocabulary test.* Circle Pines, MN: American Guidance Service.

Yopp, H. (1995). A test for assessing phonemic awareness in children. *The Reading Teacher, 49*(1), 20–29.

Yopp, H. K., & Yopp, R. H. (2000). Supporting phonemic awareness development in the classroom. *The Reading Teacher, 54*(2), 130–143.

Index